7.13.78

The Environment of Man

RICHARD N. T-W-FIENNES

ST. MARTIN'S PRESS   NEW YORK

Copyright © 1978 R.N.T-W Fiennes

All rights reserved. For information write:
St. Martin's Press Inc., 175 Fifth Avenue, New York, N.Y. 10010
Printed in Great Britain
Library of Congress Catalog Card Number: 77-26881
ISBN 0-312-25699-X
First published in the United States of America in 1978
Library of Congress Cataloging in Publication Data

Fiennes, Richard.
  The environment of man.

  (Biology and environment)
  Includes index.
  1. Environmental health. 2. Human ecology.
I. Title.
RA565.F53   362.1'04'22   77-26881
ISBN 0-312-25699-X

Printed in Great Britain

CONTENTS

INTRODUCTION

Environment of Man is the eighth of the Croom Helm series of mono-
graphs on Biology and the Environment. The first volume, by this
author, was a straightforward review of the principles of ecology as
applied to the history of the earth. The second volume by J.L.
Cloudesley-Thompson applied ecological principles to terrestrial
habitats, and was followed by two volumes by C. F. Hickling and
E. J. Ferguson-Wood on the ecology of aquatic habitats. The fifth
volume, by Robert L. Snyder, reviews the natural ecological safeguards
which control excessive growth of population and discusses how these
are operative in relation to the human race.

Snyder's volume introduces man to the ecological scene and leads
to the monograph by L. Harrison Matthews on the relationships
of man with wildlife. In the seventh volume, Sir Cedric Stanton Hicks
introduces us to the effects of agriculture on the ecology of the earth.

The present volume takes us further into the realms of human
ecology. Much has been written of the dire effects of human activity
on the earth's habitats, where . . . every prospect pleases, and only
man is vile'. I have here attempted to assess the problems, with which
man has been faced during the past fifteen thousand years or so; how,
in order to survive, he has been launched on an inflationary course;
how there is no escape from this course; and how he may shape his
future. Along the inflationary path, new obstacles arise at every
turn. The way of the human transgressor is hard.

Richard Fiennes
February 1978

1 LONGEVITY IN MAN AND ANIMALS

It is often supposed that there is some predetermined age to which animals will live under wild conditions, provided that they can avoid predators and the destructive tendencies of man. That this is not the case will be clear to those who have studied other volumes of this series, especially Volume I, *Ecology and Earth History*. Indeed, the rules of ecology preclude it, namely that population stability is maintained by the production of excess young, of which only those most fitted to the conditions of the habitat survive. The human race—in its more advanced condition—comes nearer to this idyllic state than do animals living under wild conditions. This is because in human communities, efforts are made to preserve all the young born, and to maintain them in health until the natural age of death. Consequently, a surprising number do survive until overtaken by senility, though equally—and perhaps equally surprisingly, having regard to the medical services available—a great many do not.

The necessity for human numbers to conform to the environment, and how this may be achieved, is argued in other volumes. If numbers become too great, obviously there will not be enough food to go round and disposal of wastes will become so big a problem that pollution will occur. Then numbers will inevitably come to be controlled in nature's way of removing the excess, as happens in natural communities, as still happens among less advanced races of mankind, and has happened during the long years of man's struggle to control the environment rather than to submit to its dictates.

This volume, then, will tell of man's struggle to dominate the environment and of the unsolved problems that remain with us, that is of the ways in which the environment affects man. Therefore, the struggle is not really against the environment, but of understanding the environment so that both it and man are ameliorated at the same time. This must be the first principle of environmental control.

Our ultimate goal then is that every baby shall be born alive and healthy, without injury to the health of the mother, and will live in full mental and physical health until the natural age of death. This immediately poses the question as to what is the natural age of death, and even why death at all?

For the foreseeable future at any rate, mortality must be accepted as a condition of life. What causes senescence is not known, and possible causes of it will not be discussed here. Ageing occurs in all groups of animals, even in those which are single-celled. We do not even know whether this is associated with time in years, the generations of cells—the number of cell divisions that have occurred—or with some other factor. It certainly varies with different animals, especially those that are warm-blooded. Dogs are becoming senile at the age of 12 to 15, horses 25 to 30, whereas some species of parrots and tortoises may live to be more than 100. The oldest trees, such as the sequoias, may be more than three thousand years old.

Man, himself, is something of a mystery, since the onset of senility is very variable. The biblical figure for man's life span of three score years and ten accords well with the average age attained today in Western human societies. However, this is the average for those who die relatively young and those who reach much greater ages. In addition, there are areas of the world, such as the Caucasian region of the USSR, where men allegedly do live to very much greater ages and retain their physical and mental powers and their virility. Whether this is due to some genetical factor of the race or is connected with their way of life or their diet is unknown. Although there appears to be *prima facie* evidence of longevity in these areas, definite proof of the real age of individuals is difficult to obtain, and there are few—if any—authenticated ages in man over 110 years. It is a natural human failing to exaggerate the age of very old people, and such ages are often based on hearsay. To be sure of an age, the following criteria must be satisfied:

(1) the existence of some acceptable document validating the date of birth;
(2) where the centenarian is dead, the existence of an acceptable document validating the date of death;
(3) certain evidence that the birth document and the death document refer to the same person.

Acceptance of many of the older statistics is made difficult, because often the son would bear the same name as the father, and birth and death certificates might refer to different persons. Maurice Ernest, after applying these criteria to recorded longevity records, could only accept that four persons had lived longer than 110 years—Mrs Anne Pouder, of Baltimore, born 1807 in London, died 1917; Mrs Anne Neve, of Guernsey, born 1792, died 1903, shortly before her 111th birthday; the Hon. Katherine Plunket, of Kilsaran, Ireland, born 1820, died 1932 when nearing her 112th birthday; and Pierre Joubert, of Quebec, born 1701, died 1814 at 113 years and 100 days. Alex Comfort studied subsequent birth records and found women above 110 years, though the case of the last surviving veteran of the American Civil War, who died at a reported age of 117 years, had not been investigated.

Longevity claims of 140 years or more in areas such as the Caucasus must be discounted, unless or until some satisfactory evidence for them is forthcoming. Regrettably, even the more sober biblical records are unacceptable for the same reason, though these are intriguing. For instance, Abraham is stated (Genesis 25.7) to have lived an hundred, three score and fifteen years. However, he was outdone by Isaac, whose days were an hundred and four score years (Genesis 25.38); Isaac was married at the age of forty and was three score years old when Rebecca bore twins, Jacob and Esau (founder of Edom). Jacob (Exodus I. 47.28) claimed 147 years, Joseph (Exodus I. 50. 22-3) 110 years. It was recorded that Joseph saw his son Ephraim's children of the third generation; he must, therefore, have lived to a great age and his reputed age at 110 years could possibly be correct. However, Moses (Deuteronomy 34.7) was reputedly 120 years old when he died; his eye was not dim, nor his natural force abated. Joshua, the son of Nun, was reputedly 110 years old (Joshua 24.29).

It is interesting that the only age that can be accepted for the patriarchs was that of Joseph, who lived most of his life in Egypt, where a strict calendar was kept. No doubt some of the more favoured of these nomadic peoples, living their desert lives under strict and frugal codes of behaviour, did commonly live to great ages.

Undoubtedly, there is an upper limit to the human life span and evidence suggests that this is in the region of 110 years. Some gerontologists believe that means could be found to extend this but, since the causes of ageing are still unknown, this is unlikely to be achieved in the foreseeable future. Ageing appears to be a feature of the living process. Even colonies of single-celled organisms, bacteria or protozoa, age with time, unless refreshed by the introduction of new strains. The metazoan organism is, after all, derived from the fusion of two original cells, from which are derived the myriads of cells with different functions that form a complex living machine. Some scientists believe that the maximum age is 'programmed' into the base cell at the time it is formed; others argue that there is a limit to the number of times that a single cell can divide, and that when this is reached ageing and death will occur; yet others think that during the wear and tear of life changes occur in the chromosomes leading to progressive loss of cellular function;

others believe that throughout life there is an accumulation of waste products, which the cells fail to eliminate. Ageing may be due to any or all of these causes, or to others not yet determined.

For our purposes, we can accept the fact of ageing and consider to what extent under different conditions of life the normal life span is reached. Has life expectation deteriorated since man ceased to live in small nomadic bands? What has been the effect of urbanisation, travel, intercommunication, the rise of medical science and so on? In fact, what have been the environmental effects on man arising from man's onslaught on the environment?

While an upper limit for age can be determined for different species, this figure does not represent the age at which the majority can expect the onset of senility leading in time to death; it will also differ from the actual performance of a population in terms of average life expectation from birth. Again, different sets of figures will be achieved, if life expectation is calculated from birth, from ten, twenty, thirty years and so on, especially in populations in which there is a heavy infant mortality. Even in modern Western communities enjoying the benefits of advanced medical science, the ideal picture is falsified because of premature deaths from causes such as cardio-vascular disease and cancer, which one supposes will in time be avoided. Furthermore, the stressing effects of crowds and modern life take their toll in imponderable ways whose effect is difficult to assess, but which diminish life expectation.

Gerontologists who wish to prolong the natural life span apart, it is the ambition of the medical profession to ensure that every child is born healthy and will survive in health to the end of its natural life span. In Western communities, this aim is on the way to achievement. Infant and child mortality have been reduced to small proportions, and persons living to 80 to 100 years are no longer a rarity. This has occurred largely during the last fifty years, but it is doubtful whether this situation can be perpetuated certainly unless the resulting population increase can be controlled within the natural resources of the globe. Two important factors must be considered. First, the amelioration of life in Western communities has been achieved partly by their own efforts and initiative; partly, also on the basis of imported food and fertilisers from other areas, where the people, two-thirds of the world's population, do not yet share in the amenities of the more advanced. Secondly, the less advanced two-thirds now rightly demand improved living standards and their share of the world's produce for populations which have increased following the introduction of modern medical techniques before food production has increased sufficiently.

These problems have been studied in earlier volumes. It suffices here to recapitulate that man's ways are not nature's ways. It is a new thing in nature that all young born should be expected to survive to the natural term of life. It is new, moreover, in the history of man since at no time, even amongst the most advanced peoples, has this ever come near to achievement, or even thought to be desirable except for a small minority of privileged persons. Human life, until recently, has been regarded as cheap and expendable. Amongst the Scythians of old, it was regarded as the height of degradation for a man to die in his bed. It may, furthermore, be questioned whether this aim is capable of achievement without race deterioration. The point has been argued in *Ecology and Earth History*, where it was seen that, in spite of appearances to the contrary, natural selection is still operative in the human races, but that it acts at a different level, namely before instead of after birth. The figures in Table 1.1, after the well-known British geneticist Penrose (1963), were quoted.

Table 1.1

1. Prenatal deaths	15 per cent
2. Of the remainder there are	
(a) stillborn	3 per cent
(b) deaths of the newly born	2 per cent
(c) deaths before maturity	3 per cent
3. Of the survivors	
(a) those who do not marry	20 per cent
(b) those that remain childless	10 per cent

At the present time, the human race appears to be overcoming the difficulties of prolonging life to its natural span, but the favourable results achieved may well be only temporary. There are even signs of a developing regard for the environment, which may result in a new ecological relationship, and in time permit man and the environment to come to terms with each other. The horrific trauma inflicted by man on the environment has been described in many works. This volume studies the ways in which the environment has reacted to man's nonconformity during prehistoric and historic times. It is a frightening story, which shows what may happen again unless man succeeds in coming to terms with the environment in which he lives.

Man is a product of adversity. Throughout his rise, he has been assailed by conditions and events which have threatened his survival.

He has risen above them, but only at the cost of great suffering. A survey of life spans at different times in history and under different conditions will make this clear. Edward S. Deevey (1960) constructed a longevity table for human beings at different times (Table 1.2).

Table 1.2: Human Longevity

	Years
Neanderthal	29.4
Upper Palaeolithic	32.4
Mesolithic	31.5
Neolithic Anatolia	38.2
Bronze Age Austria	38
Classical Greece	35
Classical Rome	32
England 1276	48
England 1376-1400 (Black Death)	38
United States 1900-2	61.5
United States 1950	70

The figures for the United States are taken from statistics, the rest from the ageing of skeletons from burial places, so that the two are not strictly comparable. Indeed, the longevities from the skeletal material would look worse if an adjustment were made for infantile mortality. Furthermore, it is well known that from Roman times onwards expectation of life was longer amongst the wealthier classes of the population. It is almost impossible to obtain accurate statistics from the more backward countries, where the expectation of life is shortest. However, it seems evident that this, in some parts, may be no more than 30 to 40 years.

Such performances seem appalling, when compared with a maximum life expectancy of 80 to 110 years. However, the figures require further analysis to place them in true perspective. If the figures for infant mortality are removed, life expectation is much improved, and indeed actuarial computations of expectancy at different ages show a progressive improvement after the age of twelve years. Thus the first twelve years of life are the most vulnerable, and once these are passed, individuals may look forward to a fruitful existence to a worthwhile age. In all communities, some will live to the natural life expectancy. The effect of medical care and high standards of living is not to increase the natural life term, but to enable more persons to attain it. Life tables commonly distinguish between 'senescent' deaths and 'anticipated' deaths, that is from causes not associated with senescence. The graphs will illustrate this point and also show the effect that better care and attention has had in increasing the number of deaths associated with senescence. Senescence deaths,

Table 1.3: Halley's Table

Age current	Persons	Age current	Persons	Age current	Persons
1	1,000	29	539	57	272
2	855	30	531	58	262
3	798	31	523	59	252
4	760	32	515	60	242
5	732	33	507	61	232
6	710	34	499	62	222
7	692	35	490	63	212
8	680	36	481	64	202
9	670	37	472	65	192
10	661	38	463	66	182
11	653	39	454	67	172
12	646	40	445	68	162
13	640	41	436	69	152
14	634	42	427	70	142
15	628	43	417	71	131
16	622	44	407	72	120
17	616	45	397	73	109
18	610	46	387	74	98
19	604	47	377	75	88
20	598	48	367	76	78
21	592	49	357	77	68
22	586	50	346	78	58
23	579	51	335	79	49
24	573	52	324	80	41
25	567	53	313	81	34
26	560	54	302	82	28
27	553	55	292	83	23
28	546	56	282	84	20

Age	Persons
7	5,547
14	4,584
21	4,270
28	3,964
35	3,604
42	3,178
49	2,709
56	2,194
63	1,694
70	1,204
77	692
84	253
100	107
Sum——	
total	34,000

The first life table was prepared by the astronomer Edmund Halley for the population of Breslau, Silesia, based on mortalities for the years 1687 to 1691. His figure 1 for age current at left refers to age at birth, so that all figures need to be reduced by 1 to conform to present usage. Only 50 per cent are still alive at age 34 and 75 per cent have died by age 59.
Source: Comfort (1965).

however, include such episodes as 'stroke', 'coronary disease', some kinds of cancer and arteriosclerosis, which as medical science advances may not always be regarded as associated with senescence; they may prove to be preventible. The obvious fallacy in these figures is shown by the early age of 40 and even much earlier at which such deaths begin to occur.

If we look at the life expectancy of wild or domestic animals in relation to the natural life term and compare it with human figures, we reach a surprising conclusion. We find that life expectancy amongst primitive human communities conforms to the normal pattern. The improved expectancy amongst advanced communities is abnormal, that is, much better than the normal. The nutritional and morbid states which reduce such human populations do not conform to the normal pattern, but the results are similar. Thus, the natural law of over-production of young, and population regulation by elimination of the less favoured is operative in these communities. A few examples of life expectation from animal communities will illustrate the point.

Figure 1.1: Survival Curves for Sheep

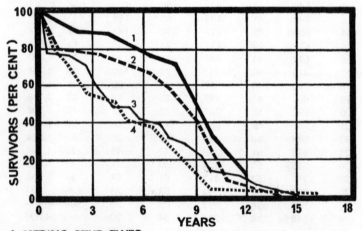

1 **MERINO STUD EWES**
2 **WILD DALL SHEEP**
3 **BARBARY SHEEP**
4 **MOUFLON SHEEP**

Sheep survival curves reflect marked variations according to environment. Valuable merino sheep fare slightly better than unhunted wild sheep. Both outlive Mouflon and Barbary sheep in captivity at the London Zoo. The latter shows a 'predator' type of curve, indicating that there is some influence from infectious diseases or population stress.

Source: Comfort (1965).

Figure 1.2: Survival Curves for Males of Five Ungulate Populations

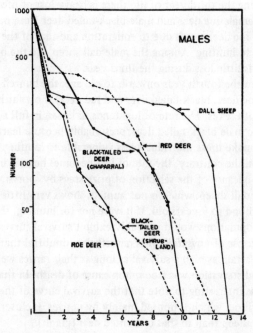

The dall sheep are not hunted. For the red deer, the older males only are hunted, when they produce fine antlers.

Source: Bourlière (1959).

All the ungulates, except the dall sheep, were subjected to hunting and this is reflected in the survival curve. However, it is worth while to quote verbatim from Bourlière, who writes:

> When we compare these survival curves, we can quite clearly distinguish some interesting similarities and differences.
> (1) A very steep initial slope, indicating a very high mortality during the first year of life, is found in both sexes of all the species. The actual mortality rate for calves is probably even greater, since their skulls are more easily overlooked and more quickly destroyed than those of adults. This age class is therefore quite probably under-represented in most samples.
> (2) During the second year of life there is small loss in both sexes of all species, with but two exceptions, that of the male roe deer where there is emigration, and that of the male black-tailed deer of

the Californian chaparral where some yearlings are killed.

(3) During the third year of life there is heavy loss of life among male and female roe deer and male black-tailed deer from both range types. The roe deer loss is due to emigration and that of the black-tailed deer to hunting. Among the male dall sheep and the male red deer there is little loss during the third year.

(4) From the fourth year onward, to old age, the hunted populations (roe deer, black-tailed deer and red deer) show fairly steep losses in both sexes. The rate of loss tends to lessen in full adulthood in the male black-tailed deer, presumably because learning and behaviour make these individuals less vulnerable to hunting. In the red deer, on the contrary, the rate of loss becomes heavier in full adulthood because of the selection of prize stags by sportsmen.

(5) The dall sheep, which is not hunted, shows very little loss from adulthood to 9 years old. If it were not for hunting, the other ungulate populations would probably exhibit survival curves more similar to those of *Ovis dalli*. It is nevertheless doubtful that they could ever attain as high a survival as long as their ranges were fully stocked and starvation was a common cause of death. In that connexion, it is interesting to note that the survival curve of the barren-ground caribou, which is hunted mainly by natives, is closer to that of the dall sheep than to that of hunted deer (graph).

(6) In old age there tends to be in most cases a steepening of the survival curve; the accelerated loss may be due directly or indirectly to senescence. In dall sheep we know, for instance, that both the very young and the very old animals were preferably killed by wolves. Heavily hunted species do not display such a pattern because the high kill permits few individuals to grow old.

The survival curves for the poorer human communities, those of India and Mexico, show a surprising similarity to those of the ungulates, which are subject to predation by man. The difference, of course, is that the predators of the human population are chronic, endemic and epidemic parasites and agents of disease. It is generally accepted by ecologists that in populations of wild animals, disease is of rather secondary importance in population control, and only becomes of significance when population pressure becomes so heavy that the animals lose their natural resistance to parasites. This might suggest that primitive urban man developed conditions of chronic over-population, a suggestion with which few would disagree. We see in both sets of curves also the high level of child and infant mortality, which appears to be a normal feature of population dynamics. In advanced human communities, infant mortality is reduced to almost negligible proportions, in striking contrast to the normal. However, in advanced human communities so high a proportion of persons either do not or cannot reproduce, so that this factor would appear to be more than counterbalanced.

Figure 1.3: Survival Curves of a German Population

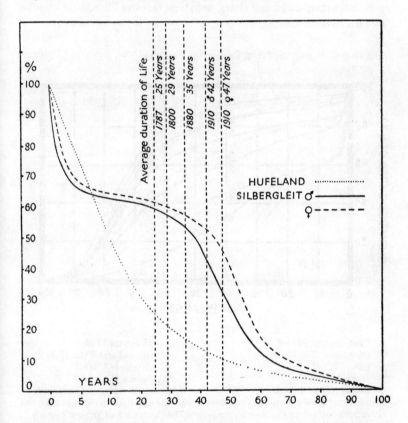

The 1798 figures resemble those for a wild population of animals subject to pre-dation. The 1915 figures show some improvement in adolescence, but thereafter resemble the same.
Source: Comfort (1956).

Comparison of the protected dall sheep with the curve for advanced human communities displays a striking difference. The dall sheep show a steeply plunging curve towards the end of the natural life span. The

human curve of senescence extends over half the natural life span from
40 years to 80 years or thereabouts. The human curve is, in fact, dis-
torted because of deaths due to the so-called senescent diseases, such as
stroke, coronary heart disease, cardio-vascular disease, disease of the
kidneys, cancer and such-like. As has already been said, all or some of
these may not necessarily be diseases of senescence. They could be associated more with unnatural features of man's ecology, such as population
pressure, urbanisation and stress, unnatural features introduced by man
into his environment.

Figure 1.4: Human Survival Curves for Females

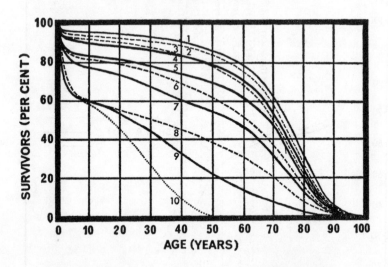

1   New Zealand 1934-8   2   US whites 1939-41
3   US whites 1929-31   4   England and Wales 1930-2
5   Italy, 1930-2   6   US whites 1900-2
7   Japan 1926-30   8   Mexico 1930
9   British India 1921-30   10 Stone Age man (guesswork)
These curves show clearly the resemblance between populations living in primitive
conditions and animals subject to predation. The figures are all 'pre-antibiotic'.
Source: Comfort (1956).

   We have, therefore, in this work to study two main unnatural elements,
resulting from man's relationship with his environment: first, the pre-
ponderance of diseases as the main population-controlling element in
more primitive communities; secondly, the emergence of the so-called
senescent diseases in those communities in which infectious diseases and
parasites are successfully controlled.

2 THE EMERGENCE OF MAN

Today's human races include a cross-section of almost all phases through which man has passed since Palaeolithic times. Palaeolithic or Neolithic cultures exist—or until recently have existed—amongst the Australian peoples, the Bushmen of South Africa, the Amerindians and the Eskimos. Early Iron Age cultures, combined with shifting agriculture, were until recently predominant amongst the negro races of Africa. Primitive urbanised situations exist in many parts of the world, including some parts of India. Our modern urbanised societies are still emerging from the traumatic effects of the Industrial Revolution, whose ills were not originally understood or controlled.

In the last chapter, we have found some interesting correlations in life expectancy curves, which it is worth while again summarising. We found that these curves conformed to those of wild animal populations under predation, but that the place of the actual predator in controlling population levels had been chiefly by a high incidence of disease combined with famines and other periodical catastrophes. Amongst the modern urbanised societies we found that the infant mortality and that from 0 to 12 years had been reduced to small proportions. We found that so many more persons survived to the end of the normal life span, that diseases of senescence appeared unnaturally early and that there was a high proportion of 'genetically unfit' persons (more than 50 per cent who did not breed or whose offspring did not breed); this, to a certain extent, redressed the balance. Amongst the less developed peoples, population and nutritional problems are more pressing. On this basis, the outlook appears reasonably rosy, provided that the less advanced peoples can catch up with the more advanced. It is only on this basis that world problems can be tackled in a uniform way, man being regarded as an element of a global ecosphere, as argued in *Ecology and Earth History* (Fiennes, 1976).

Today, man is emerging, after a transitional phase, into a totally new type of environment of his own creation. He is still learning how to come to terms with this new environment, a process which involves profound changes in his way of life, changes which are at variance with his natural instincts and which impose damaging restrictions on him. Our ancestors of the late Palaeolithic era, only twenty thousand years ago, were nomadic creatures and we are still driven by nomadic urges. Our standard of physical health is better than ever before, we do not lack for food, we enjoy unprecedented luxury and ease of living, and yet we are probably more discontented than our forebears ever were. We continually seek new ways of 'escapism'; the 'whodunnit', the 'box', travel, excursions, the weekend cottage, the boat and the 'hippies'; perhaps even religious outlets are an expression of the nomadic urge. Frustration of this urge is surely responsible for many of our social difficulties. Satisfaction of it would surely lead to greater contentment and reduce other symptoms, such as industrial unrest, withdrawal types of mania, resort to alcohol and drugs, suicides, and the unnatural pursuit of wealth or power as an end in itself. In all these ways, modern man reveals his nonconformity with his new environment, but as he has created it he must come to terms with it. In this chapter, we shall try to see how this situation has arisen in such a remarkably short space of time.

J.D. Bernal has likened the impact of post-Mesolithic man on the environment to a new evolutionary force. A similar idea was expressed in *Ecology and Earth History*, when we included man's agricultural revolution amongst the major turning points in earth history.

However, taxonomically man has not evolved. He is still *Homo sapiens*, indistinguishable from his Cromagnon ancestors, who hunted over the sub-arctic tundra. The change is a change of behaviour forced by the impact of a suddenly changed environment. In time, measured in tens of thousands or hundreds of thousands of years, possibly evolution will produce a species of *Homo* that will be anatomically and physiologically more adapted to a settled existence, but it may be argued that elimination of the restless qualities that made man might not be beneficial to his survival notwithstanding. For perhaps three million years, the human race lived in open country, in the sub-arctic tundra of the Ice Age and the open Saharan plains of the African pluvials and elsewhere. As a highly sophisticated and intelligent hunter, he fitted into the ecological habitat, a habitat he was forced to adopt when desiccation in his pre-hominid phase of evolution made him leave the forests where his ancestors had lived. Having become adapted to the open country, he came to fear and avoid the forests. With the change of climate at the end of the last Ice Age, forests appeared on his ancient hunting grounds, and a change in his way of life became inevitable. Such had happened before during the intermissions ('interstadials') of the Ice Age, and palaeontological evidence shows that at such times man's numbers diminished. On this occasion, man acted differently—and radically. He reacted against the environment in a way so novel as to open a new page in earth history.

It all started with a new invention. After thousands of years spent in making stone tools of increasing sophistication, man invented an axe, the 'polished stone axe'. He seems to have been acutely aware of the importance of this invention, the symbolism of which has come down to us from ancient mythology. As a weapon, it was borne by the horse-riding Battle Axe Folk of Neolithic central Asia. It was passed by them to the Beaker people, who copied it in copper. It had symbolic attributes for the Minoan people of Crete, and was the symbol of the Nordic god, Thor. It was symbolically carried by the Roman lictors in their fasces. In England, the oldest bodyguard of the sovereign, the Honourable Corps of Gentlemen at Arms, adopted it as their symbolic weapon in 1526 AD. A symbolic axe, in the form of the halberd, is still the arm carried by the Swiss guard at the Vatican.

As a weapon, the axe is of limited value. However, it enabled Meso-lithic man for the first time to attack the trees of the forests in an effective way. Once this was achieved, the Mesolithic age quickly gave way to the far more sophisticated Neolithic, and thence to the Chalco-lithic (copper) and Bronze ages. Not only were forest areas cleared and used for agriculture, but timber also became available for manufacture into useful articles. Flints and other stones were adapted to a large number of uses and the forerunners of many of our carpenters' tools were devised in stone to work the felled timber. Saws were made by fit-ting flint teeth into wooden frames; polished stone adzes were natural successors to the axes; chisels of stone were devised, and as a natural development from them even planes. In this way, not only could timber be felled, it could be worked. Boats, and even ships, could be made. Wheels, carts, wagons and chariots followed.

Furthermore, the ability to obtain timber in quantity made possible the burning of charcoal, and so led to the smelting of metal ores and paved the way to the Chalcolithic, Bronze and Iron ages.

The earliest agriculture appears to have been practised in the mount-ainous areas surrounding the 'fertile crescent' of Mesopotamia. Tree growth was first cleared so that agriculture too was dependent on the invention of the axe. It was only later that crops were grown by irrigat-ion in the great river valleys. At the same time, man's reduced mobility led him to herd and then domesticate some of the animals he had formerly hunted, and in this he was aided by the dogs he had domestic-ated from the wild wolf stocks. And so the nomadic hunter became the settled agriculturist with all the profound consequences that followed.

Not all human tribes were forced to abandon the nomadic way of life.

Great plains remained, stretching from Siberia to the Black Sea. On them were large herds of horses and other plains animals which continued to be hunted. On these, man retained his nomadic way of life until recent times. Paradoxically, these nomadic peoples eagerly adopted newer technologies, and throughout the ages continually assaulted and replaced the settled peoples of more southern regions. They proved fully as inventive and more skilled in the use of military weapons. They domesticated horses and used them at first for riding. They then invented the wheel and developed wheeled transport. They built carts and wagons to which they yoked oxen. From the solid wheel, they developed the spoked wheel and so armed themselves with horse-borne chariots. Furthermore, they became adept at working the new metals and made swords and spears superior to those of the southerners. As chariotry or cavalry, the horse was to be the foremost military weapon until the First World War, so that these 'barbarians' continued to threaten the settled areas of the world for a very long time. Even the Greek and Roman infantry formations required light cavalry to protect their flanks and rear.

The response of the nomadic peoples to civilised advance shows that man was intellectually equipped before Mesolithic times to challenge the environment; it needed the spur of climatic change to induce him to do so. He must also have been intellectually equipped to develop science and technology long before he actually did so; otherwise, how were advances in these spheres so quickly made? In astronomy and mathematics, notable advances were made in Egyptian, Babylonian and Grecian times. In social science, the laws of Hammurabi and the precepts of the Hebrews were on the whole humane and enlightened. However, the advance of scientific thought and method was stifled from Pharaonic to recent times by conservative forces in the form of all-powerful priesthoods, superstition and dogma. Furthermore, the continuous overthrow of the early city-states by untutored invaders made continuity of philosophical thought almost impossible.

The earliest forms of agriculture were based on the cultivation of wild wheat and barley in Europe and the Near East. In the Middle and Far East, rice was also cultivated. The earliest form was nomadic or 'shifting' agriculture, but settled systems quickly followed in the great river basins, where systems of irrigation were developed. The nomadic agriculturists gradually migrated across Europe to Scandinavia in their search for fertile land capable of being worked by their primitive tools. In more northern lands, wheat and barley grew less well, but crop contaminants, oats and rye, thrived abundantly and so became the main crops. Nomadic agriculture, therefore, led to dispersion, an important feature; the new Stone Age displaced the Mesolithic in the Near East in a few hundred years; it reached Scandinavia after some two thousand years. However, the virile peoples living there reacted to it rapidly and dramatically, as we shall see. Released from the restrictions of Mesolithic times, their nomadic instincts drove them to become amongst the world's greatest travellers and traders.

Settled agricultural systems were developed along the Nile, Tigris, Euphrates and Indus valleys. They led to the development of permanent settlements, then to cities, city-states, kingdoms and empires. The easy acquisition of food led to division of labour (and of wealth), cultivation of the arts and sciences, trade and trade routes, dispersion of knowledge, banking and accounting and so to writing; also to insecurity, greed, crime and warfare. It also led to the difficulties and dangers associated with crowded and urbanised existence.

However, let us first follow our nomadic agriculturists. These peoples used four main tools: the polished stone axe, with which they could clear an area of woodland; the digging stick, used to make holes for the planting of seed; a flint-toothed sickle, used to reap the crop; and a stone quern, with which the grain was ground after winnowing with leafy branches. Once the ground was cleared, the vegetational debris was burned over the area and the seed planted below the ash. Only one, or at most two, crops could be successfully raised in this way, and then another site needed to be cleared. Such sites have been studied in Scandinavia; good accounts are given by Braidwood (1960) and Iverson (1956), including accounts of modern attempts to grow the primitive grains by these methods. This method of life represented an adaptation of man's former nomadic existence to changed circumstances and provided sustenance for a limited number of people. The diet was supplemented by hunting and gleaning vegetable foods in the forests, and some domestic animals were also being kept. However, these migrations opened up communications between the northern peoples with their wanderlust and the prosperous river-based agricultural communities of the south with two far-reaching and major effects. The Scandinavian peoples quickly developed trade routes with the south, based on the great European river systems. They learned to build both river and seagoing boats and thus started the great Neolithic trade boom (see Bibby (1962)). Second, the still-nomadic peoples of the Asian and European steppes had developed a distinctive culture of their own based on the horse. Armed with superior weapons—they were fine metal craftsmen once the Neolithic gave way to the Chalcolithic (copper) and Bronze ages—and horses, they continually raided and overthrew the

luxury-loving, city-dwelling peoples of the south. This they continued
to do until the horse-borne invasions of Genghis Khan in the fourteenth
century AD, and of Tamerlaine a century later. Settlements of the early
Neolithic period were open; those of the late Neolithic were fortified.

The river-based civilisations achieved great prosperity. They traded
amongst each other as far as the Indus, and caravans wound their way
from Babylon to China. Cities and markets arose along the caravan
routes. Some states and dynasties survived for a few hundred years,
protected by the great walls of their cities, as with Babylon, or by military prowess and tyrannical ferocity, as with the Assyrians. For all the
writing was on the wall. Sooner or later the conqueror was at the gates;
a quick death for those of the males who were lucky; for others to be
flayed alive or impaled; slavery and concubinage for the women. In this
new environment, man was his own predator. In these cities, a high
degree of luxury was achieved and life was undoubtedly comfortable.
Laws were, on the whole, fair to all, and standards of hygiene probably
better than in Europe during the Middle Ages. Disease and pestilence
do not seem to have been a major problem; possibly the periodical
burning of the cities was beneficial.

Except in Egypt, the ancient irrigation works have long since perished. In time, the soil became impregnated with salts from the irrigation
water, rendering them infertile—a long-term victory for the environment.
Watersheds were denuded of timber; the rainfall lessened; run-off became
more severe; erosion and aridity made the land infertile. Alone in Egypt,
the Nile annually renewed the soil, so that crops have been continuously
harvested there, since those distant days. Here, too, however, the environment struck back. The waters of the Nile became infected with the snail-
borne disease of bilharzia, one of the most prevalent and debilitating
diseases known. The vigour of the population was sapped by this liver-
living worm and Egypt became an easy prey to the invader.

The Greeks, a race of philosophers, like our Victorian ancestors saw
clearly the abuses of their age but did nothing about them. They destroyed their watershed timber and dried up their numerous springs. They
left a legacy of philosophy and science which survives to this day, and,
influenced by the Egyptians, they laid the foundations of modern medicine. Belatedly, the small Greek cities and states combined to meet the
Persian invader, and at the battle of Marathon made military history
that led to the subsequent supremacy of Rome. For the first time, the
chariot charge was defeated by the heavy infantryman, the Greek hoplite.
The Persians did not read the military lesson and a century later at the
Battle of Gaugamela, the Greek hoplites organised as the 'phalanx' under

Alexander of Macedon broke Darius' chariot charge and the Persian Empire fell to the Greeks. The Roman legion was evolved from the phalanx and the Romans at long last were able to control the horse-borne hordes of the north and conquer and stabilise the Mediterranean world.

When the fabled Alexander died in Babylon, probably of typhoid fever, at the early age of 33, his short-lived empire split into two. His general, Ptolemy, made himself Pharaoh of Egypt with his capital of Alexandria. Another general, Seleucus, founded the Seleucid dynasty which ruled a vast empire from Antioch to India. The Greeks were great traders, more interested in trade than conquest. There does not seem at this stage to have been great abuse of the earth's resources. The Sahara still supported a population of nomadic pastoralists, and Egypt became the greatest grain producer of the world. The bitter struggles of earlier days had left most of the land in good heart, and history does not record widespread famine and pestilence. Wars and religious practices served to control populations and man himself had outlets for adventure. There had, hitherto, been no irreparable outrage done to the environment except on a local scale. All this was changed by the Roman conquests. The Romans ravaged and exploited the earth for the sake of their own small city and the territories around it. In their heyday, their luxury and pride and their degradation were unsurpassed. In the long run, they destroyed their country, their peasantry, their agricultural lands, their watersheds, their soils, and their culture. The story has been told in another volume by Sir Cedric Stanton Hicks (1975). At the end, they destroyed their people too, when disease and pestilence came to dominate their country and left them defenceless. Not only this, but the whole civilised world was left defenceless at the mercy of the peoples of the north and the steppes, which the legions had kept at bay. The world receded into ignorance, poverty and disease, dominated by an unenlightened priesthood. The experiment in civilisation, which had started so hopefully in Neolithic times, collapsed dismally within a century or two of the decline of the Roman Empire. Environmental forces, abused and exploited, hit back and centuries passed before man began to recover from the blow. Nomadic man had triumphed over agricultural man.

In history as it is related, we hear of the great conquerors, of Rameses and Ashurbanipal, of Alexander and Hannibal, of Quintus Fabius Maximus—'Unus qui nobis, cunctando restituit rem', of Scipio and Caesar. We hear little of Imhotep, Asclepios, Hippocrates, even of Aristotle. We hear little of Tiberius Gracchus, who foresaw the dangers to agriculture in Latium and Tuscany and was murdered by the Roman Senate for advocating land reform, nor of Varro and Columella, who wrote sound treatises on Roman agriculture. Yet, early farmers had sympathy with their soil and knowledge of it. They knew how to rotate crops and of the value of manure and legumes. Plato knew that the water sources in Greece were dry because of tree removal from the watersheds. The foundations of medicine and hygiene had been soundly laid. The deliberations of Aristotle and other philosophers had laid the foundation of scientific observation and experimental science. Even the tenets of dogmatic religion were questioned by the Greeks. So, why was it that a promising start had to collapse, and to collapse in so drastic a manner that the lessons learned were forgotten for hundreds of years?

Evidently, man was on the horns of a dilemma. Agriculture and urbanisation had been forced on him by environmental change, but he was basically a nomadic animal and not an urban one. The early urban settlements fell easy prey to nature's darlings, the nomadic peoples who lived on and by their environment. Rome, following in the footsteps of Alexander, for a time made urban environments secure. But populations grew and could only be supported by exploitation of conquered territories; exploitation of the homelands followed, which rendered them agriculturally useless. What then was the solution? Rome had no answer, except to grow in grandeur and degeneracy. Maybe at the time there was no answer. If there was, it would have taken a Greek to find it, not a Roman. But a Greek would have been incapable of founding an empire like the Roman; otherwise, the Greeks would have done so instead of submitting to Roman conquest. Here is the dilemma; that wise advance into the future must be in conformity with an avenging environment; and such an advance can only be made if all the nations of the world are of one mind. Rome could only make them of one mind by conquest, and even so lacked the necessary knowledge of long-term consequences and foresight.

The situation in the world today is not unlike that which prevailed at the end of the Roman era, but with important differences. We have enlightenment and knowledge, and we know—or can discover—what needs to be done. We have developed the scientific approach, by which we can predict the results of our actions and devise means to overcome unfavourable consequences affecting the environment in which we live. To win the support of all the peoples of the earth for such measures, or even of all the people living in one country, may be as difficult as in Roman times. We have to relieve the poverty of the impoverished, the ignorance of the uneducated, and the prejudices of those to whom a

quick dollar is more important than impoverishment of future generations. Finally, we still have much to learn about health and disease,
about nutrition and the behavioural requirements of urbanised man.
Indeed, we are still, in spite of our advances, ignorant of the requirements of the environment we have created and in which we aspire to
live. This is not surprising, as they plainly vary according to the stage of
culture that has been reached.

Two types of situation require to be considered: first, that which prevailed from the time when man began to live in crowded settlements;
second, that which has come to prevail and is developing, since the great
advances of medicine and hygiene during the past hundred years. Combined with the latter, account must be taken of social advances, which
have enabled most people in advanced societies to enjoy an income that
is adequate for a high standard of nutrition and reasonable periods of
rest and leisure. The former phase was—and is for all but a few privileged
areas of the world—transitional. The latter phase too is still transitional
in that, since its inception, new problems have appeared requiring sol-
utions. In the former phase, man did not understand his environment;
in the latter, man is coming to understand it; he is conscious of the extent
to which he is defiling the environment and of the rate at which he is
squandering natural resources, on which he is dependent and which, once
depleted, cannot be replaced. He is also becoming aware of many ways
in which his activities and his effluents are damaging to his own and
other species of living things.

Limitation of deaths leads eventually to limitation of births. This in
turn leads to an urge for survival—not survival of the fittest, just survival. So, we contrive the survival of deformed or genetically incapacit-
ated children, mongols, anencephalics and so on; we keep alive artificially
those whose brains have been destroyed by accident, and old people who
would be better allowed to die peacefully. In former times, life was not
regarded with such deference and those who died prematurely did so
with the comforting thought that life was a burdensome prelude to a
nobler and happier existence elsewhere. The decay of such beliefs makes
it seem the more important to preserve both one's own life and the
lives of others, since it is the only time one will experience it and have
one's own individuality. If so, why take heed for the future? Live for
the day and let future generations look after themselves. If there will be
no more petrol in twenty years' time, all the more reason to enjoy your
motoring while it lasts. In these ways, man's emerging mastery over
environmental problems is having important psychological as well as
physical effects. Indifference to problems could be as disastrous as

ignorance of them. This is why, in *Ecology and Earth History*, we stressed
the importance of philosophical and religious enquiry as well as techno-
logical. Since revealed religion came under the searchlight of science,
leaders of religion appear to be in complete bewilderment with no idea
of how or where to look for confirmation of the religious truths they
preach. An understanding of human ecology and the physics of matter
could help them.

In other volumes of this series, it has been suggested that, for purposes of human ecology, the earth be regarded as a single ecosphere. In
a way, this idea may seem absurd, because environments and habitats
differ so greatly in areas where human beings live. Climates are different;
vegetation is different; disease and health problems are different; and
people are different. Nevertheless, these are all places where human
beings live and multiply, and where they must come to terms with the
problems which face them. In the next chapter, we shall take a look at a
rather new branch of medical science, that of geographical medicine. In
the space available, the review can be only cursory but will throw some
light on modern environmental problems. It is an area of research to
which the World Health Organization has contributed greatly, showing
that man *can* combine to tackle problems on a global scale.

3 GEOGRAPHICAL MEDICINE

The great advances in medical science came with the use of the microscope and the discovery of bacteria and other organisms of disease by pioneers such as Pasteur and Koch. In earlier ages disease was associated with 'Airs, Waters and Places'. Even so, a simple exercise in medical geography had enabled Dr John Snow in 1849 to attribute an outbreak of cholera in London to infection of the water of the communal pump in Broad Street. Jenner, too, evidently recognised the infectious nature of smallpox when he immunised his patients with cowpox vaccine. However, both Snow and Jenner earned the ridicule of their colleagues of the medical profession. Snow overcame the ridicule and proved his point by removing the pump handle. Jenner was eventually justified by success.

However, if you believe that diseases are a function of Airs, Waters and Places, the obvious approach is to study them geographically, an approach which in this sense is as old as Hippocrates. This approach is entirely justified, since diseases undoubtedly are associated with places, and both air and water are common agents for their transmission. With the development of microbiology, knowledge of the actual agents of disease came rapidly and the science of immunology followed. However, the application of pharmacology to diseases of temperate climates lagged behind its application to tropical diseases in the refinement of such drugs as quinine for use against malaria, the arsenicals for sleeping sickness, and antimonials against leishmania and bilharzia. Sulphonamides, antibiotics and other anti-bacterial drugs were only developed more than fifty years later. Furthermore, the natural history of disease advanced more rapidly in tropical countries with the discovery by Ross of the transmission of malaria by mosquitoes and by the work of British and German scientists on the transmission of sleeping sickness by tsetse flies.

This situation highlights the fundamental difference between disease patterns in tropical and temperate climates. In hot countries many diseases are transmitted by insects and other intermediate vectors, which do not thrive so well in colder countries where they must pass the winter in hibernation or in the egg stage while still retaining infection. In the tropics, not only protozoa and helminth parasites are transmitted by vectors, but also a large and important group of viruses, the arboviruses

31

of which yellow fever is an important example. Insect-borne and similar diseases have a debilitating effect on the population, and account for the deaths of up to 20 per cent of children before puberty. The effect is more serious in settled populations in proportion to the numbers, because in such conditions the population of both parasites and vectors becomes larger and more concentrated. The effects on small groups of people who keep moving will be correspondingly less. It may well be supposed that these factors of disease were to a large extent responsible for preventing peoples in tropical areas from settling in large groups or— where they did—in undermining their stamina to such an extent as to frustrate the full development of their faculties. The local inhabitants developed some resistance, not shared by immigrants from temperate regions, who died like flies in the 'white man's graves':

Beware, my son, the Bight of Benin,
whence few come out, though many go in.

This is seen not only in the human populations, since domestic stock are equally at risk, and their loss from disease, famine or other causes contributes to shortages of food, especially protein, and thus to diseases, such as kwashiorkor, which increase the loss of stamina and performance of the people.

Much as the colonial era was disliked in tropical countries, this phase was undoubtedly indispensable to the people. For how else could these disease problems be studied and mastered and the people brought to a state of health and vigour in which they could order their own development?

The earliest advances in civilised living occurred in the Mediterranean basin, and it is tempting to suppose that this occurred because the Mediterranean climate is that most suited to man's performance. This theme has been developed by Gordon Manley in his book, *Climate and the British Scene* (1952, 1962 and 1970). Manley, a lawyer and at one time secretary to the British Prime Minister, Ramsay Macdonald, pointed out that the earliest centres of civilisation occurred along the 70° F isotherm, and that this happened not only in Europe, but also in the Americas, where civilised states were developed by the Aztecs and Incas, but nowhere else. He reckoned that civilisation only effectively moved northward when advanced heating methods were developed. Thus, as with the African situation, there were limitations to advance also in Europe and Asia, but the solution was more easily found.

It could be argued also that the 70° F mean isotherm line represented the area where grains suitable for domestication existed, wheat, barley, rice and maize, and that Manley's correlation was not with climatic suitability for man, but with the grains. Nevertheless, the Mediterranean basin and comparable areas in South America and the Middle and Far East do represent the warmest parts of the earth, where a temperate rather than a tropical disease pattern prevails. Thus closer settlement was possible without the dangers of universally acquiring chronic debilitating diseases. However, the correlation is likely to be as much with seasonal variations of temperature as with the mean. There are many areas in tropical Africa with comparable *mean* temperatures, but owing to lack of variation throughout the year, parasitic vectors of disease do not have an interrupted growing season.

Problems posed by the river-based irrigational systems of agriculture were primarily due to the snail-transmitted diseases caused by trematode worms. Those prevalent in Africa are bilharzia (*Schistosoma haematobium* and *S. mansoni*; in the Far East *Clonorchis sinensis*). The eggs of these worms are passed in the urine in the case of *S. haematobium*, and in the faeces in the case of *S. mansoni*. *Clonorchis* infects cats as well as man, and the snails acquire larval infection from cats' faeces; however, a second larval form passes from the snail into a fish and man acquires infection by eating the fish. To eliminate bilharzia, therefore, is simple; you do not urinate or defaecate in water. In Egypt, the form of bilharzial infection is *S. haematobium,* resulting from the urine, but it is virtually impossible to prevent all the *fellahin* working in irrigation areas from contaminating the water. In any case, the dangers arising from urination into water have only recently become known.

Whereas, therefore, the development of city-dwelling in sub-Saharan Africa may well have been physically prevented by disease hazards arising from close settlement, in the river-based settlements close settlement was initially possible but debility and a decline of vigour in the people followed secondarily from their agricultural practices.

Civilisation in temperate areas got off to a reasonably good start, hazards of warfare apart. As early as Minoan times, there were forms of water-based sanitation. The Sumerians had deep pit latrines lined with earthenware pipes. The Romans built their Cloaca Maxima and flushed latrines with buckets of water. Furthermore, the cities were small, perched on tops of hills, and the peasant population lived on farms surrounding them; only when the invader came did they take refuge within the city walls. Mycenean settlements were of this type and so were Iron Age Celtic, such as Maiden Castle. Throughout Greek and Roman times the system seems to have worked reasonably well, though, as we have seen, the Romans undermined their civilisation by a social system which could not endure. It was after the collapse of Rome that the world was swamped by Germanic and Nordic peoples who, unused to city life, turned cities into dunghills, rivers into sewers, and lived in a stench which must have been unbearable. Such conditions became steadily worse until the middle of the eighteenth century, when belated steps were taken to manage sewage and water supplies.

As can be supposed, medical conditions were deplorable. Rats abounded and spread plague, notably in the great epidemics of history; the Black Death in the fourteenth century killed half the population of Europe, and a heavy toll was taken by the Great Plague of 1665. The Enclosure Acts in Britain led to the peasantry being driven off the land and into the cities, and the Industrial Revolution led to the development of slums and appalling living and working conditions in the enlarged cities. Cholera, enteric, dysentery and other intestinal infections were rife. Tuberculosis was almost the rule rather than the exception. The death rate was phenomenal in rich and poor alike, though the poor suffered worse.

Rural areas were affected by the decline of the Roman roads system. Villages were cut off from each other to such an extent that a local food shortage might lead to famine and death, although a village twenty miles away had a food surplus. Furthermore, marriage between close relatives became so common that genetical defects and idiocy were widespread.

Improvement came slowly and conditions only changed radically with the invention of the anti-bacterial drugs and antibiotics during the Second World War. By their use, deaths from pneumonia and tuberculosis were to a large extent eliminated and the mortality statistics became radically changed, deaths from infectious causes giving pride of place to the so-called senescent diseases and the expectation of life becoming markedly extended. The situation had, of course, improved greatly and progressively from the mid-nineteenth century onwards, due to improved sanitation and communications. However, it was not until antibacterial agents were freely available that every child born had a reasonable chance of living in good health to the natural age of death.

In one way or another, whether in tropical or temperate areas, environmental factors associated with an unnatural way of life have impeded human progress in ways that are only now coming to be understood.

Hand in hand with industrialisation, there has appeared a new group of diseases, those known as 'occupational'. Today, these are the concern of industrial medicine, and factory laws continually take account of new processes used and of a greater range of chemicals used in industry. The effects of some may be immediately apparent; with others, the effects are delayed, perhaps cancer in middle or later life. With others, as with lead and mercury, cause and effect may not be readily apparent. The traditional 'mad hatter' suffered from neurological changes resulting from the chemicals used to smooth the hats. Perfume workers at Grasse in France suffer liver damage from the essences of perfume distillation. Silicosis has long been associated with mine-workers; and today the even more dangerous asbestosis is all too common in persons working with asbestos used in the brake linings of cars. The general public, too, is at risk from agricultural, aerial and water-borne pollution in ways that are only now coming to be studied and controlled.

During man's history, the geography of medicine has not only been apparent in the distribution and incidence of infectious diseases. Nutritional problems have been at least as important if not more so. Whereas a great deal is now known about the control of infectious diseases, it can be argued that real understanding of nutrition is less far advanced. Some observers believe that the diet of agricultural and urban communities lacks the variety of that consumed by man's Stone Age ancestors. Agriculture is largely a method of making starch, so that with a monotonous diet large quantities of starch must be consumed to provide a sufficiency of nutriments required in small quantity but too highly diluted in agricultural products. This situation leads to diseases of civilisation, such as obesity and hardened arteries. In some parts of the world, where the diet is reasonably good, as in Ethiopia, people keep fit and perform their daily tasks adequately on a calorie intake which would be regarded as grossly inadequate in Western countries. 2022283

Primitive man found in wheat a grain of high value with a protein content of some 15 per cent and a satisfactory content of the essential amino acids. He quickly learned to supplement this with beans and other legumes, of which the protein content is even higher. As a dietary staple, therefore, wheat is satisfactory, but the same cannot be said of staple goods developed, particularly in tropical countries, where wheat will not grow. Such staples are the millets, sorghum, cassava, sago and bananas. Even maize and rice are less satisfactory than wheat. The disease of kwashiorkor, mentioned above, is rife throughout tropical countries, particularly in children. This disease is due to a deficiency of protein in the diet, and is associated with swollen belly, progressive wasting, and disease of the liver. Mental faculties are retarded and death eventually occurs. The symptoms are reversed when adequate protein is added to the diet. Where the people supplement the basic starchy diet with fish or meat, or even beans, the disease does not occur. However, where such luxuries are scarce or reserved, as in times of famine, for the adult members of the household responsible for the heavy work of agriculture, the children are deprived.

It was not only in tropical countries that dietary problems arose. The existence of famine in English villages cut off from their neighbours has already been noted. At the beginning of winter in more northerly areas, as in Scotland, many of the cattle were slaughtered and the meat salted because of lack of winter feed. The people too had little to eat as winter progressed and vitamin deficiency diseases, especially rickets and scurvy, began to appear, though their association with deficiencies of diet was not known. There was little milk, few eggs, and no green vegetables until the spring. Vegetables were, indeed, scarce in winter even in prosperous households right up to the First World War. The rapid appearance of scurvy in ships' crews was an indication of how short the winter diet was in vitamin C. This shortage was partially alleviated when potatoes were introduced. Not only are potatoes a valuable food, rich in protein, but even today they are the major source of vitamin C for the majority of the population. Even so, the older potatoes eaten in winter contain less vitamin C than do younger ones of the early crop. Nutritional diseases, then, were a debilitating factor even in temperate climates, and the short stature of the poorer people was probably associated in no small degree with a periodical absolute shortage of food. Such shortages would, of course, render the people even more susceptible to infectious diseases. Shortage of vitamin D, present in milk, butter, eggs, fish and liver, led to the development of rickets in a proportion of persons to whom these foods were not available. In the summer, the shortage would be less marked because of the effect of sunlight in synthesising it in the skin. However, such an effect was diminished in the big smoky cities, through the atmosphere of which the ultra-violet rays were less able to penetrate. Just how marginal the intake still is of vitamin D is shown by a renewed incidence of rickets in dark-skinned immigrant children in Britain at the present time.

The geographical incidence of disease distribution is used today for the study of the causes of disease. Where there is a high incidence of a particular disease in a certain area, then special factors may be looked for in those areas to account for it. In Derbyshire—and many other areas in the world—there is a high incidence of goitre, due to enlargement of the thyroid gland, known as 'Derbyshire Neck'; this condition is due to a deficiency of iodine. Iron deficiencies lead to iron-deficiency anaemia. Shortage of fluoride in the water leads to caries and tooth decay. There may be a number of other deficiencies of minerals required in trace amounts, the effects of which are not yet known but require study.

One of the more interesting associations, not yet understood, is the relationship of cardio-vascular disease with soft water. In hard-water areas, deaths from diseases of the cardio-vascular system, such as coronary heart disease and stroke, are statistically lower than in soft-water areas. Experiments have failed to reproduce this effect in experimental animals, such as pigs and rats, so what property of the hard water contributes to the lowering of this incidence is not known. It is generally supposed that this might be one of the elements present in hard water, rather than the hardness of the water itself. Such might be zinc, vanadium, magnesium, molybdenum, or some other element.

Cardio-vascular disease, at present classed as a disease of senescence, today precedes cancer as the major cause of death. Changes in the arteries are found in young men in their twenties and thirties. Yet in more primitive peoples it either does not occur or is very rare. Is this a racial characteristic or is it related to dietary habits? Evidence suggests that it is related to diet. There is a Western-type incidence amongst Arabs in Israel, whereas outside Israel the incidence is low; the Israel Arabs consume a Western-type diet, the others their traditional diet. The high incidence amongst Western peoples has been variously attributed to their high intake of cane sugar, to their consumption of solid fats instead of oils, sedentary habits, and so on. Disease of the cardio-vascular system may well prove to be preventible; if so, much misery and distress could be avoided and the life tables would look much better.

The second-highest cause of death in Western societies is cancer. There are many different types of cancer, some of which may be analysed by geographical medicine. Cancer of the cervix in women has a lower incidence in races which practise male circumcision. From this, it is argued that the cause is infection, probably a virus, and that the virus is present in the male smegma which accumulates below the prepuce (the foreskin). Other cancers have a high incidence in certain areas, and causal factors are sought for them peculiar to those areas. A typical example of successful geographical sleuthing was that of the Burkitt Lymphoma.

The Burkitt Lymphoma is an eroding tumour of the jaw bones which occurs in tropical areas, particularly in Uganda, where it was investigated by a British doctor, Dr Denis Burkitt, after whom it is named. It affects young children of ages 8 to 12, and rapidly results in death. Attempts at surgery were unsuccessful, though it can now be cured in some cases by suitable drugs. Dr Burkitt noticed that these tumours only

occurred in those areas of Uganda where malaria was endemic. He therefore supposed that the tumour was caused by some infectious agent,
probably a virus, whose effect was enhanced by malarial infection. A
virus has since been isolated from these tumours by two British scientists,
Drs Epstein and Barr, which belongs to the herpes group of viruses and
which in other areas causes glandular fever.

To complete this short review of geographical medicine, it is necessary
to study the subject of man/animal relationships—the diseases of man
that can be transmitted to animals (anthroponoses) and those of animals
that can be transmitted to man (zoonoses). These are of two types, those
arising from contact with wild animals, and those arising from contact
with domestic animals.

All wild animals carry some burden of parasites and potential pathogens, which may take their toll between weaning and puberty or in
old age. The general adult population comes into balance with them, so
that they are not harmful, unless stressing factors such as food shortage
or over-population become established. These remarks apply as equally
to primitive human communities as to other animals. Many pathogens
and parasites are spread directly from one animal to another by direct
or indirect contact, indirect contact being by way of contaminated soil,
vegetation or tree bark and so on. In such an event, usually only one
species is host to the parasite. However, there is a form of relationship
between prey and predator species, which is important to parasite transmission. In its simplest form, this is seen in the transmission of the common tapeworm of Canidae, including domestic dogs. The adult tapeworm lives in the gut of the canid; eggs are passed in the faeces and con-
taminate pastures; the larvae are consumed by grazing animals, deer or
sheep; the larvae form cysts in the abdominal cavity of the grazer. If
the herbivore host is killed by a dog or a wolf, the tapeworm cyst is
eaten and the predator acquires infection.

A particularly nasty tapeworm is a minute parasite of dogs, known
as *chinococcus granulosus.* Although the adult tapeworm is minute, the
larval cyst—known as 'hydatid'—grows continuously and becomes enor-
mous; it becomes attached to the secondary host's liver or other organs,
which may be largely destroyed. The secondary host may be a sheep or
a horse or a donkey—or man. This worm has become a major danger at
sheep-shearing stations as far removed geographically as Wales and
Australia. When the sheep are brought in for shearing, those that are
infected with hydatid may die or be killed because they are in poor
condition. The carcasses are then given to the sheepdogs, which become
heavily infected with the adult worm. It is very easy for the sheep shearers

to get their hands contaminated with the dog's excreta in such situations, and in this way they can acquire hydatid, unless they are careful about washing before they take a snack.

Man's own natural predator/prey relationships are with cattle and pigs, which harbour the cysts of human tapeworm in their muscles— known as 'measles'. Infection can only reach these animals if infected persons defaecate in the pastures where they graze. Man is infected by eating the meat, which is not rendered safe by normal cooking proced- ures. In Western countries, tapeworm infection is rare because stand- ards of personal hygiene are high and beef and pork are inspected at abattoirs. In less advanced countries, the infection rate may be high, though the worms do little harm. However, pigs in some areas also have a high infection rate with a roundworm, called *Trichinella spiralis*. This worm encysts in the muscles, and if the flesh is eaten infects the muscles of the person eating it. This parasite can cause severe muscular pains and distress in breathing because it gets lodged in the respiratory muscles, and people sometimes die as a result. It is sometimes said that taboos against eating pork originally arose because the dangers of this parasite were recognised.

The conditions so far mentioned are those associated with normal predator/prey relationships. They do not normally become widely dis- tributed or necessarily dangerous except in special circumstances, as with the sheep-shearing situation, or where intensive agriculture leads to an unnaturally high degree of stocking. In two other types of sit- uation, zoonoses can be much more dangerous: first, in population explosions of wild animals, where they tend to migrate and their nat- ural bacteria and viruses cause active disease under the stress; second, when there are unnatural contacts between species that normally live apart.

The well-known lemming migrations are a typical instance of the first type of hazard. Lemmings normally carry, as a normal commensal, the bacterial agent of a serious disease of man known as tularaemia, caused by *Pasteurella tularensis*. When the migrations occur, the lem- mings in great columns migrate over fields and through villages; some die and some are eaten by dogs and birds and invariably there are out- breaks of 'lemming fever' amongst the human populations. The great outbreaks of plague, which occurred periodically from Roman times throughout the Middle Ages, were associated with massive migrations of the black rat from the Far East; they not only swarmed over the land surfaces, but got into ships and so were distributed all over the old world. The causal agent, *Pasteurella pestis*, is a normal commensal of voles and other rodents; infection was passed to the black rats, which began to die and migrated. Rabies is another instance of this type of situation. In some areas it is endemic in wild carnivores, such as foxes and skunks or in bats. Domestic dogs become infected from the wild carnivores, and man is at risk from the dogs.

Unnatural contacts between man and dangerous animals have become more frequent because of the importation of exotic species as pets, or for research. Many deaths have occurred from psittacosis acquired from parrots. Deaths of children have occurred from salmonella infections acquired from imported tortoises. Skunks can be unaffected carriers of rabies. However, the most dangerous animals to man are those most closely related to him, his fellow primates. From them can be acquired such diseases as bacillary and amoebic dysentery, B. virus infection, Marburg Disease, infectious hepatitis, tuberculosis and rabies. Many people have died as a result of contact with these animals. Under jungle conditions too, unnatural conditions can fortuitously occur. Yellow fever is transmitted in the jungle from monkey to monkey by mosquitoes, which normally live high up in the trees. The monkeys in most areas are unharmed by it. However, if woodcutters fell a tree in the forest, they may be bitten by infected mosquitoes which come down with the tree. The virus can then pass from the infected person into certain domestic mosquitoes and an epidemic with numerous fatalities may be started. Many more examples could be cited.

The geography of medicine, therefore, has many facets. Man has created many unnatural situations with the result that unusual problems have continued to arise, by which the health and performance of his peoples have been threatened and impaired. It has been possible in this brief survey to give only the barest outlines of the subject, though certain aspects will be elaborated in succeeding chapters. In the next chapter, we shall look in greater detail at the nutritional problems of civilisation, which may be less well understood than those of infectious disease.

4 PROBLEMS OF NUTRITION

Man's agricultural revolution probably had little immediate effect on his well-being. However, once the change from nomadism became absolute, the adoption of a staple diet of grain posed many problems, which were not understood and are only beginning to be understood at the present time.

Seeds, as a source of food, had been exploited by no group of animals, except seed-eating birds and to a lesser extent by very small rodents. Even the seed-eating birds consume insects also during the breeding season. Unless produced in mass by agricultural means, the seeds are wasteful in time for collection and it would be difficult to collect enough to feed so large an animal as man and his family. The seeds of herbage are undoubtedly consumed by grazing animals, but their chief source of sustenance is the leaf and not the seed. Furthermore, the starch grain cannot be digested by non-herbivorous species because of its cellulose sheath. Therefore, it must be cooked either by boiling or by prolonged steaming. The use of grain as a staple food requires it to be grown in sufficient quantity for harvesting, winnowing, grinding and cooking.

Many grains contain a reasonably high content of valuable protein. For instance, hard wheat—that which was first domesticated—contains some 14.0 per cent. Others are of less value and some of the starch roots, potatoes excepted, are grossly deficient. Even the best grains contain too little protein and too much starch to be ideal for human consumption. In primitive societies, cereal gruels are normally given to children at six months old; such gruels may be made from sorghum, maize, cassava, or other starchy foods, containing no more than 8 per cent of protein of poor biological value. A child, for example, will require 1.1 kilograms of rice to meet its calorie requirements, and this amount of rice will provide only 22 grams of protein against a minimum requirement of 30 grams. However, the appetite is satiated before so much rice has been consumed, and the protein will be used as part of the calorie requirement and not for tissue building; this is the order in which the body meets its priorities. Energy requirements are met before protein requirements. At the same time, the child's weight and bulk appear to be unimpaired, because fluid is retained. In such societies, breast-feeding is often continued until the end of the second year of the baby's life, and the breast milk is essential for its proper growth and development. Even so, numbers of babies suffer severely from mal-nutrition, due to the 'protein/calorie syndrome', attributed by President Nyerere of Tanzania to 'poverty, ignorance, prejudice and disease'. We might reflect that this is a hangover of the agricultural revolution and the adoption of new food sources that are not understood.

During the first year of life, then, conditions of straightforward calorie deprivation occur amongst infants. They are seen chiefly amongst primitive peoples, where the mother lacks sufficient milk, but are not un-known in industrial countries in babies on formulated feeds which are too dilute. This condition is known as 'marasmus', another word for starvation; the baby wastes away but recovers when the calorie intake is augmented.

Symptoms of protein, as opposed to calorie, deprivation may occur from the sixth month onward if breast-feeding is discontinued. This frequently occurs because of tribal taboos if the mother becomes preg-nant again. The cereal diet given to the child requires to be supplemented with meat, fish or legumes, but where these commodities are scarce, this is rarely done. The child then develops the disease of kwashiorkor—more simply protein starvation. The disease was first described in the Gold Coast (now Ghana) by Dr Cicely Williams in 1933. Kwashiorkor is the word in the Ga language meaning 'the sickness of the deprived child'! Even so, the true significance and the cause of kwashiorkor were not realised until 1956. This was partly because the deprived children became very susceptible to parasites, such as hookworm and other dis-eases, which were formerly believed to be the cause, partly because in relation to size and weight the children did not show obvious signs of starvation. In kwashiorkor there is cessation of growth and the muscles are wasted, but these symptoms are masked because of a massive retent-ion of water. Such children, unless treated in time, suffer permanent impairment, both physical and mental, and may die. Mental changes may be indifference, irritability or apathy, and a sadness of expression. There is also chronic drowsiness. Physically, the hair changes colour and may be reddened. The skin shows decreased pigmentation. There is diarrhoea and depletion of potassium and magnesium. Affected children are also anaemic and have impaired heart function. Liver changes, due to lack of protein, lead to cirrhosis.

Such are the kinds of problems, as they affect young children, associated with the changes of feeding habits that arose with the agricult-ural revolution. They are world-wide but occur especially in tropical countries where the grains and other cereal sources of food have low

Figure 4.1: Infant Feeding Patterns Leading to Marasmus and
Kwashiorkor

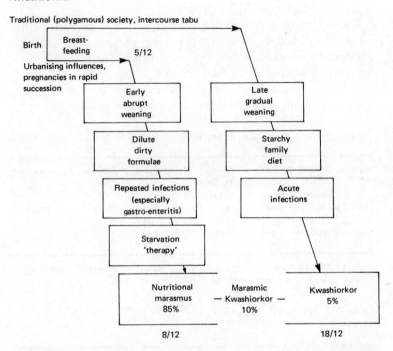

Early weaning, a feature of urbanisation, leads to marasmus. Prolonged breast-feeding leads to kwashiorkor. Numbers represent approximate age in months. Percentages of types of malnutrition are based on figures for Jordan, but are typical for
many other countries.
Source: Robson (1972), p. 106.

Table 4.1: Quantity of Cooked Cereals Required to Meet the Calorie
Requirements of a Two-year-old Child

Food	Amount (kg)
Maize gruel	1.53
Maize dough	1.60
Sorghum	1.59
Rice	1.10

Source: Robson (1972).

protein contents. Added to the high exposure to tropical disease, they
constitute a threat sufficiently severe to undermine the stamina of entire

tribes or races. These diseases are rarely, if ever, seen amongst the surviving nomadic Stone Age peoples whose subsistence may be frugal but is varied and high in good-class protein.

The lack of diversity in post-agricultural revolution diets has led to many other difficulties, which affect not only primitive peoples but advanced communities as well. The varied diets of Stone Age man necessarily contained all the food factors that were needed. Many are the diseases associated with deficiencies of vitamins and minerals that have only recently become recognised or remain unrecognised. As a

Table 4.2: Per Caput Availability of Protein and Calories in India 1960-6

India	Cereals	Potatoes	Pulses, Nuts, Seeds	Milk	Protein	Calories	Protein cals %
	g/day	g/day	g/day	g /day	g/day		
1960/2	383	29	63	127	49.6	2020	2.45
1963/5	380	35	54	117	49.1	1960	2.5
1965/6	456	39	41	110	45.4	1810	2.5

Protein calories are 2.5 per cent against a minimum requirement of 4 per cent.
Source: *State of Food and Agriculture*, FAO, Rome, 1968.

Table 4.3: Per Caput Availability of Protein and Calories in Tanzania 1960-2

Protein	58.1 grams
Calories	2080
Protein cals %	8.9

Protein calories are 8.9 per cent, which is adequate.
Source: *State of Food and Agriculture*, FAO, Rome, 1968.

corollary to the diseases of deprivation, let us study one of the major diseases of advanced communities, namely 'obesity'. Obesity, and one may suspect diseases of the heart and arteries that often go with it, is as surely a symptom of the unnatural feeding habits of post-agricultural man as are deficiency diseases.

Obesity results when the energy absorbed from food sources exceeds the body's energy output. Energy derived from excess input is stored as fat and to a lesser extent as animal starch, or glycogen, in the liver and muscles. Energy output is threefold: first, that required for basal metabolism, maintenance of body temperature and basic functions such as

Figure 4.2: Trends in Food Production and Population in Developing Countries

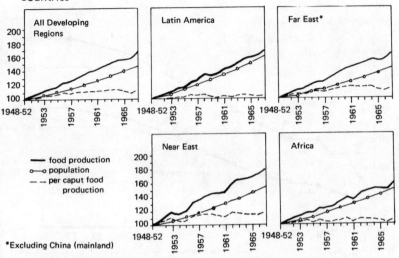

In 1966, per caput food production decreased. The situation reveals one in which under-nutrition is likely amongst the poorer classes.
Source: *State of Food and Agriculture*, FAO, Rome, 1968.

Figure 4.3: Reference Protein Requirements by Age

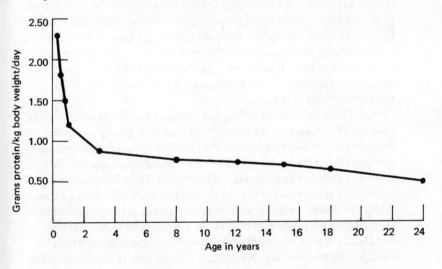

Source: World Health Organization Technical Report, Series No. 301, 1965.

Figure 4.4: Protein Requirements and Recommended Dietary Allowances by Age and Sex

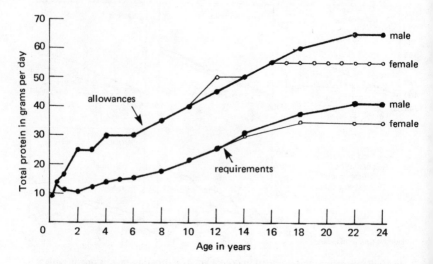

Source: World Health Organization Technical Report Series, No. 301, 1965 and *Recommended Dietary Allowances*, Seventh Edition, National Academy of Sciences, Washington, DC, 1968.

cardiac and respiratory movements; second, the specific dynamic action of certain foods, which stimulate energy production; third, that required for the daily activities of life. Provided that energy input is balanced by output, obesity cannot occur; furthermore, all slimming routines are based on the reduction of energy input below that of output, in which case calorie requirements are supplemented from the energy stores; therefore, obesity is reduced.

Agriculture has been described as a means of producing a high-energy food, starch, cheaply; in other words, to provide the body's calorie requirements. However, it ignores the necessity to provide a multitude of other substances, such as protein, vitamins, minerals, essential fatty acids, and so on, in high enough concentration. Therefore, when a predominantly starchy diet is consumed, it is necessary to consume excess calories to obtain repletion with these requirements; thus, where high-energy foods are freely available, excess calories tend to be consumed and obesity results. The position is worsened by the sedentary lives led by most city-dwellers, which leads to a reduced calorie requirement. For a creature with the digestive and metabolic apparatus of man, the mainly cereal diet is, therefore, unbalanced; it has even been suggested that man's primitive diet was so low in carbohydrates that his body is very retentive of them and readily converts them to fat. The position is worsened by modern agricultural practices, which have led to the production of low-protein grains and high-starch roots and piths, such as cassava and sago. Hard Manitoba wheats still possess a high protein content of some 14 per cent; in British wheats the protein content is around 8 per cent, and in many wheats used in the manufacture of cakes and biscuits the protein content is very much less. At the same time, consumption of bread is diminishing and that of cakes and biscuits is increasing. A further loss of valuable nutrients occurs during the milling and processing of grains, so that cereals become less and less satisfactory. This is to a certain extent overcome by 'fortifying' bread flour, which is required by law in most advanced countries. By this means, some of the lost vitamins and minerals are restored to the bread. British breads, made from British and Manitoba wheats and fortified with the more obvious essentials, are an excellent food and not too blameworthy as a cause of obesity. The same can be said of potatoes, which are reasonably high in protein and when not too old very rich in vitamin C. However, many people are afraid to consume these foods for fear of obesity and often deprive themselves of their valuable constituents or consume other foods with higher energy contents, and less valuable composition. Some young people, in fear of becoming obese, deprive themselves of energy-containing foods to the extent that they suffer from starvation. Furthermore, it is known that a balanced intake of the right kind of fats together with carbohydrates will to an extent prevent their conversion to fat by the body.

Table 4.4: Protein Calorie Percentages of Common Staples

Food stuff	Protein cals %
Sago flour	0.6
Cassava flour	1.8
Plantains	3.1
Sweet potatoes	5.3
Irish potatoes	10.7
Rice	8.0
Maize flour (whole meal)	10.5
Wheat flour (white)	11.4
Sorghum	11.3

This shows how inadequate in protein are many vegetable foods. Even where the protein calories are adequate, the amino acid content is likely to be deficient.
Source: Robson (1972).

Table 4.5: Protein Food Mixtures

Product	Country	Composition	Protein content %	NDpCal %
Incaparina	Guatemala	Maize, cotton seed flour, vit. A, lysine $CaCO_3$	27.5	7.4
Pronutro	South Africa	Maize, skim milk, peanut, soya, fish protein concentrate, yeast, wheat germ, vit. A, thiamine, riboflavin, niacin, sugar, iodized salt	22.0	
Saridele	Indonesia	Dry soya, sugar, $CaCO_3$, thiamine, folate, ascorbic acid	26-30	
Arlac	Nigeria	Peanut flour, skim milk, salts, thiamine, riboflavin, folate, vit. D	42.0	
Indian Multipurpose Food	India	Peanut flour, chickpea flour, $CaCO_3$, vit. A, thiamine, riboflavin	40.0	
C.S.M.	USA	Maize, soya flour, skim milk, $CaCO_3$, vitamins	20.0	10.8
Laubina	Lebanon	Wheat, chickpea, sesame, skim milk, minerals, vit. A and D, thiamine, riboflavin, niacin	16.0	7.8

This table shows how adequate diets can be compounded from vegetable foods. Source: PAG Bulletin No. 7, *Amer. J. Clin. Nutr.* 17: 143, 1965, and Proc. Seventh Int'l Congr. Nutr., 4: 152, 1967.

The obesity problem is by no means as simple as is suggested by the energy input/output formula and there is plainly still much that is not known about it. A genetical factor appears to be involved. Fat children are often the offspring of fat parents. Furthermore, if babies up to three years old receive excess calories, this has a permanent effect in making them obese in later life. In order to absorb the excess calories, their bodies make more fat cells, which are retained throughout life and always mop up any excess energy available. It is, therefore, as unwise to overfeed a baby as to underfeed it. An important factor is the control of appetite, probably a hormonal feedback mechanism. Some people have large appetites and some small. To an extent, appetite can be trained or conditioned, and one of the objects of slimming régimes should be to re-educate the appetite, so that the most suitable foods are demanded once the régime is ended. However, what are suitable foods is a question on which no two authorities seem to agree. The body reacts to foods in somewhat unexpected ways. For instance, cane (or beet) sugar is split by digestion in two halves; one half is glucose and the other fructose (fruit sugar). Although they are both 6-carbon sugars varying slightly in chemical composition, the fructose moiety, which is the sweeter tasting, is quickly converted by the liver to fat whereas excess glucose is oxidised to carbon dioxide (CO_2) and water (H_2O) and excreted, providing the body with energy requirements in the process. Some years ago, it was found that, if carbohydrate calories were replaced by fat, obese patients lost weight, and the 'Eat Fat and Grow Slim' cult arose. If the fat given was in the form of hard (saturated) fat, this could be a most dangerous proceeding, as will be discussed below. The effect of the fat is probably to give a sense of satiety, whereas its sheer bulk is more than can be digested so that much of its energy content is never absorbed into the body.

The obesity problem, like that of marasmus and kwashiorkor, appears, therefore, to be one of imbalance between calories, proteins and other dietary essentials, coupled with a low energy output. The obvious solution is to reverse the trend away from high protein grains. Alternatively, our unnatural grain foods should be fed to animals, which can convert them to more suitable food. This, of course, we do in stock husbandry, and no doubt primitive man did this to a greater extent. However, populations have risen to such an extent that this is becoming increasingly difficult, and meat is becoming so expensive as to be out of reach of many people. Furthermore, natural grazing lands are becoming more limited and intensive rearing and gathering régimes are necessary. Under these, the quality of the meat is diminished; it contains more hard fat and water and its nutritional value is reduced. Even natural herbivores cannot make protein from a high carbohydrate diet, nor can they make soft (unsaturated) fats from carbohydrates; they require fresh vegetation.

Whether a fully satisfactory vegetarian diet can be devised for human beings is to be doubted. Vegetarians and vegans will argue the point. The difficulty lies chiefly for those between 0 and 20 years, when protein demands are high and exacting. Much bulk is required to provide sufficient calories, and the protein intake lags behind the calories, as we have seen. However, it is not really the protein which is crucial, but its constituent amino acids, the substances from which body cells are largely built, from which are manufactured the immune bodies which protect from disease; proteins also are the great transporters of vitamins, fats and other substances to sites where they are required. There are eighteen amino acids, of which nine are essential; this is to say that the body must have them and cannot convert them from others. The body selects the amino acids it needs and discards the rest. Proteins are, therefore, used wastefully and must be given in excess so as to allow for this selection and they must be of a quality to provide the amino acids needed. Animal proteins have a much higher 'biological value' than vegetable, which are deficient usually in several essential amino acids. Wheat flour is the best or would be best but for the low protein grains now being grown. However, much better results in respect of amino-acid balance can be obtained if grains are mixed so as to achieve the best possible amino-acid balance. In this way, the requirement of animal food supplements can be greatly reduced and a greater understanding of this approach is important for the future. Much can be done further by supplementing vegetable diets with beans, peas and pulses, and in respect of fat requirements—not so far discussed—with oil seeds and nuts.

Another limiting factor in the purely vegetarian diet is that of fats and oils. This has been little understood until recently, when rapid advances are being made. Saturated fats serve merely as energy stores, for insulation of the body against cold, for protection of vulnerable points, such as joints, and for giving it attractive contours—especially in women! The unsaturated fats are structural elements of all body tissues and cell membranes, especially of the brain and other nervous tissues. They are essential in energy transfer mechanisms, are the precursors of important hormones, the prostaglandins, and assist as transporters of substances such as cholesterol, which in their absence will accumulate in the arteries, skin and other places. Owing to the large bulk consumed, vegetable foods can provide herbivorous animals with their needs of unsaturated fats. Even so, it is claimed that these fats serve as limiting factors to brain development, and that no purely herbivorous animal could produce a brain of the relative size of a human one. Therefore, carnivorous animals, or mixed feeders such as man, must obtain these fats at least in part from animal sources. It is suggested that this is one reason for the existence of the otherwise wasteful prey/predator relationship on the ecological scene. In the absence of animal food, persons relying on a solely vegetarian diet will slowly deplete their reserves of long-chain unsaturated fats and a mother will be unable to supply her unborn baby with its requirements for brain growth. The child will be mentally retarded, and the situation will be even worse for the child of the second and succeeding generations. These are suppositions, which cannot yet be regarded as proven, but they could be important in assessing their possible effects on the performance of backward peoples. Indeed their importance is such that it is worth while to give some study to the theoretical implications.

The saturated fatty acids are simple carbon structures with the following formula:

$$\text{(methyl end) } CH_3 - CH_2 - CH_2 - CH_2 \text{ COOH (carboxyl end).}$$

There may be any number of carbons in the chain. Fats are formed by linkage of fatty acids with an alcohol, the alcohol in living systems being glycerol. The unsaturated fatty acids are deficient in one or more of the hydrogen atoms, so that there is a double bond linking the carbons. The empirical formula will then appear as under:

$$CH_3 - CH_2 - CH = CH - CH_2 ....COOH.$$

There may be any number of double bonds situated in any position, except that there cannot be two double bonds adjoining. There are, in fact, only two 'families' of unsaturated fatty acids important in living systems, linoleic (C18: 2 n-6), and linolenic (C18: 3 n-3). Linoleic acid is an eighteen-carbon acid with two double bonds, the first of which is situated at the sixth carbon from the methyl (CH3) group. Linolenic acid is also an eighteen-carbon acid, but with three double bonds, the first being situated three carbons from the methyl group. Though these acids are manufactured by plants, they cannot be synthesised by animals. The animal body can, however, lengthen the chain by adding additional carbons and can introduce additional double bonds, but this can only be done at the carboxyl end of the molecule. Linoleic and linolenic acids are, therefore, the essential base substances from which more complex molecules can be made. In the structure of brain and other nervous tissue, heart, muscle, skin, the coats of red blood corpuscles and other tissues, there occur both linoleic and linolenic acids and 20- and 22-chain acids also. Deprivation particularly of linoleic, probably also of linolenic, results in serious deficiency symptoms affecting the nervous system, the liver, the skin and hair, the testes or ovaries, and other tissues. In the young, many of the symptoms are not reversible, so that deficiency in a child may lead to permanent impairment of mental faculties, sterility and other abnormalities. As with many deficiency states, deprivation is probably in most cases partial, so that the results may not be fully apparent. In the long term, the unsaturated fatty acids have the property

of lowering blood cholesterol because this substance can only be trans-
ported when attached to them and to protein. Since cholesterol is a
major component of the atheromatous plaques which formed in arteries
are the precursors of coronary heart disease, long-term partial deprivation
of these fats may well be implicated in the etiology of cardio-vascular diseases. Furthermore, it is known that they play some part in the mobilis-
ation and use of the saturated fats. The high ratio of saturated/unsatur-
ated fat in the diet in urban societies is thus likely to be an important
contributory factor to the early onset of senescent diseases.

All fats and oils contain some proportion of unsaturated fatty acids.
In fats, such as cream and butter, dripping or lard, it is so small as to be
insignificant. In lean meat, liver and fish, it is high and chicken breasts
and skin are a rich source of linolenic acid. Whereas animal foods mostly
contain the two 18-carbon essential fatty acids or their higher derivatives,
vegetable oils—all rich in unsaturated fatty acids—vary in their content
of the two essentials and never contain longer-chain ones. Thus corn
oil—as everybody knows today—is rich in linoleic acid, but it lacks linolenic; the same is true of sunflower and safflower oils. Linseed oil is very
rich in linolenic acid, but has little linoleic. Soya bean oil, on the other
hand, contains both linoleic and linolenic acids, about the only vegetable
oil to do so. Olive oil contains only oleic acid, having only one double
bond and, therefore, of no value for dietary purposes. Olive oil, however,
is exceptionally rich in the oil-soluble vitamin E (alpha-tocopherol),
which plays a special part in the metabolism of the essential fatty acids.
Growing shoots and green leaves are the richest sources of linolenic
acid, as opposed to the seed oils, mostly rich in linoleic, lettuce leaves
have high value.

The unsaturated fatty acids, by their chemical structure, are very
vulnerable to oxidation; that is, they easily become rancid even at
refrigerator temperatures. Linolenic acid, having three double bonds,
is more vulnerable than linoleic and is therefore usually excluded from
proprietary margarines and vegetable oils. Oxidation occurs at the
double bonds and the chains split into substances with a distinct colour
and an unpleasant odour. The pure acids are odourless and colourless,
even that of linseed. These oils would become rancid so quickly as to
become worthless, unless they were protected by anti-oxidants, of which
a number are available to food manufacturers. However, nature provides
its own anti-oxidant, vitamin E, which is present to some extent in all
vegetable oils, and especially in olive oil. Vitamin E is an essential dietary element for all animals, without which metabolism of the essential
fatty acids cannot take place. Furthermore, the liver cannot handle these

acids in the absence of another vitamin of the B group, pyridoxine.

Linoleic acid is today widely incorporated in formula feeds for babies, cooking oils and margarines. Both linoleic and linolenic acid are abundant in hens' eggs (more in range-fed) and in human breast milk. They are deficient in cow's milk, which is a poor baby food both in this and other respects. They lose little of their value in the normal processes of cooking and can be readily incorporated in dressings such as mayonnaise. Their increasing use should in time be reflected in improved health of urban populations. However, the knowledge of their properties is so recent that no assessment can yet be made, and only a small proportion of the population is as yet aware of these properties. It is still, also, thought that incorporation of linolenic acid is unnecessary. This view almost certainly requires to be modified.

The inherent dangers in man's switch from the diet of a nomadic hunter to that of a sedentary agriculturist relying on a cereal staple should be abundantly clear from what has been written. However, little has yet been said of other essential dietary items, such as the vitamins, minerals and trace elements, ignorance of which has led to disease and suffering throughout recent human history.

The vitamins comprise a group of organic chemicals, which are essential to important metabolic functions, but which the body cannot manufacture. They must, therefore, be obtained from external sources, that is from vegetable or animal foods. Alternatively, some can be synthesised by microbes which inhabit the bowel. Thus, herbivorous animals in particular are well placed to obtain those vitamins from the organisms concerned in their digestive processes, and to pass them on to animals which prey on them. Also, vitamin deficiencies commonly occur when drugs or antibiotics are used to control infections if they eliminate some of the intestinal flora. In many ways, the vitamins resemble hormones produced by the endocrine glands. Hormones—or chemical messengers as they are called—control important bodily processes, being produced by the endocrine glands in response to specific stimuli. Vitamins perform the same kind of function, but they must be constantly present either in the products of digestion, which the body absorbs, or in reserve stores in the liver and other tissues. Both vitamins and hormones have certain so-called 'target' organs on which they produce their effect and which in their absence suffer from structural or functional defects.

There are two main groups of vitamins: first, those which are soluble in oil or fat; second, those which are soluble in water. Between these two groups there is an important difference. Those that are soluble in

Table 4.6: Summary of Functions of Vitamins and Manifestations of
Vitamin Deficiencies

Vitamin	Function	Characteristics of the Deficiency State
Fat Soluble		
A	vision, membrane structure, health of epithelia, bone formation, reproduction, growth, synthesis of mucopolysaccharides, glycogen and RNA	night blindness xerophthalmia keratomalacia bone malformation growth retardation
D	calcium absorption, mobilisation of calcium from bone, phosphorous retention, citric acid oxidation	rickets
E	antioxidant, cellular respiration, heme synthesis	anaemia
K	blood coagulation, oxidative phosphorylation	haemorrhage
Water-Soluble		
ascorbic acid	formation of collagen and dentin, oxidation of phenylalanine and tyrosine, utilisation of folic acid and iron, synthesis of progesterone, neutrotransmitters and catecholamines, cellular respiration	scurvy
thiamine	carbohydrate metabolism	beri-beri
riboflavin	biological oxidation-reduction reactions	cheilosis, glossitis, angular stomatitis, eye changes
niacin	biological oxidation-reduction reactions	pellagra
pyridoxine	amino acid metabolism	anaemia, convulsions, dermatitis
biotin	fixation and removal of carbon dioxide	dermatitis, muscle pain, anaemia, somnolence
pantothenic acid	transfer of acyl groups and maintaining rate of phosphorylation	cramps, depression, insomnia, burning sensation in feet
folic acid	transfer of single-carbon compounds	megaloblastic anaemia
B_{12}	synthesis of single-carbon compounds	pernicious anaemia
choline	constituent of lecithins, sphingomyelin and acetylcholine, methyl donor	fatty liver in animals
inositol	constituent of certain cephalins	weight and hair loss and fatty liver in animals

Source: Robson (1972).

fat can be stored in the body, so that temporary or even quite prolonged deficiency in the diet will not induce symptoms if reserves are high. However, a constant intake of the water-soluble vitamins is necessary to maintain health, because any surplus intake is quickly excreted. For this reason too, the water-soluble vitamins can be consumed in any quantity within reason without harmful effects, whereas over-consumption of the fat-soluble vitamins can have dangerous consequences.

Amongst wild communities of animals, there may plainly be dangers of seasonal vitamin deficiencies when food is scarce. These dangers are nothing compared to those arising from monotonous and unvaried diets and purified foods. It is those dangers to which man has been exposed during the years since he came to live by agriculture. The effects have been profound and the stamina of whole races has been threatened at times, because one or other of the vitamins has been lacking from the diet. To what extent partial deficiencies are responsible for ill-health, in the absence of clinical symptoms, even in Western societies, cannot be assessed with any reasonable degree of accuracy; evidence would suggest that they are medically important. However, before reviewing the medical importance of these deficiencies in human history, let us cursorily study the main vitamins involved.

The fat-soluble vitamins are: (1) vitamin A, of which the precursor is carotene; (2) vitamin D—or calciferol; (3) vitamin E, or alpha-tocopherol.

Vitamin A

Carotene, the precursor from which the body manufactures vitamin A, constitutes the colouring matter of vegetable foods, such as carrots, sweet potatoes and sweet peppers, all of which are a rich source. It is also present in fish and fish oils, meat and liver. Even so, deficiency of the vitamin is widespread in all countries of the world. One reason may be that it cannot be absorbed from the bowel in the absence of fat or oil in adequate amounts. People living on a dry diet of grain in some form may well suffer from deficiencies, even though their intake of carotene in supplementary foods would appear adequate, unless they are consuming enough fat (saturated or unsaturated) in some form. Evidence of deficiency can often be seen in African peoples, to whom sources of the vitamin are readily available in sweet potatoes or other foods, probably for this reason. The vitamin is required for maintaining the integrity of epithelial (surface covering) tissues in all parts of the body, with the result that a wide variety of organs, lungs, kidneys, bowel and skin may be affected in deficiency states and the patients' resistance to infections is lowered. The symptoms most readily seen are in the skin and the eyes. The skin is dry, pale and scaly. The eyes suffer from a characteristic form of ophthalmia known as xerophthalmia, in which the cornea becomes hardened. The vitamin is also concerned with manufacture of the pigment, rhodopsin, which becomes bleached in the eyes in the dark, and assists night vision. Persons suffering from deficiency, therefore, also suffer from night blindness, though this may also be due to other causes.

Vitamin D

Vitamin D is obtained largely from the same sources as vitamin A. It is responsible for the absorption of calcium from the bowel and for its utilisation in the body in bone manufacture and maintenance and for maintaining the calcium at the required level in the blood. If blood calcium is lowered, symptoms of tetany appear, from which the consequences can be serious. How it performs these functions is a very complicated story, the whole of which we still do not know. Vitamin D is also manufactured in the skin from a substance present there known as ergosterol; however, this only occurs when the skin is exposed to ultraviolet light. The characteristic disease associated with vitamin D deficiency is rickets, in which bone growth is impaired. This has been very common amongst children in smoky cities, and is today frequently encountered in coloured immigrants, probably because the ultra-violet light of the sun is trapped by the pigment in the skin.

Vitamin E

Vitamin E is present in greater or lesser amounts in vegetable oils, in which—as we have already seen—it plays a part in preventing oxidation, that is rancidity, developing. In the body, it also has an essential role in the metabolism of the essential fatty acids, and in its absence they are incapable of utilisation. Lack of vitamin E is associated with infertility and muscle atrophy.

The water-soluble vitamins comprise the B group of 12 or more vitamins, vitamin C, vitamin F and vitamin K. Where one of the B vitamins is deficient, others are likely to be deficient also. Gross and widespread deficiency of B_1 (thiamine) followed the practice of consuming polished rice in the rice-eating communities of the Far East. The resulting disease of beri-beri affecting the nervous system undermined the stamina of whole communities and babies born of deficient mothers were also sufferers. As serious in maize-eating communities was the disease of pellagra, due to lack of vitamin B_2 (nicotinic acid). This disease is associated with loss of weight, gastro-intestinal and mental disturbances and skin lesions.

Deficiency of others of the B group (riboflavin and pantothenic acid) also result in skin conditions. Vitamin B_{12} and folic acid are essential for blood formation and in their absence a form of anaemia occurs. Folic acid is also important in maintaining pregnancy.

Vitamin C appears to have multiple importance. Gross deficiency leads to the well-known disease of 'scurvy', in which there are changes in the bones and teeth and haemorrhages occur from rupture of small capillary blood vessels. It, too, appears to be concerned with essential fatty acid metabolism, possibly as a water-soluble anti-oxidant supplementing the role of vitamin E as a fat-soluble anti-oxidant. Large daily doses appear to have an effect in removing excess cholesterol from the blood, possibly also from atheromatous plaques in arteries, perhaps due to greater activation of essential fatty acids. It is also claimed to have an effect in protecting people from the common cold. This is a vitamin likely to be in short supply in winter diets, when the intake of fresh vegetables and fruit is diminished. Potatoes are fortunately rich in vitamin C and supply the major intake in countries such as Britain. Scurvy was the scourge of sailors in the old days of the windjammers, though it came to be learnt that a daily intake of lemon juice would prevent it. Most of the sailing ships used to carry dried peas as an article of diet; if the masters had only known it, these would have produced abundant vitamin C if placed on the deck and watered to produce shoots. Vitamin F is necessary for milk production by nursing mothers, and vitamin K is necessary for blood clotting.

This very brief survey of the vitamins will serve to highlight the dangers to health that arose when agricultural man turned to diets lacking variety. Indeed, whole communities throughout human history have had their health undermined by such deficiencies, resulting in frank and identifiable diseases or subclinical conditions that are not so easily recognised. No less important is the intake of mineral elements required either in gross or trace quantities. The importance of salt (sodium chloride) has been known from earliest times. Lime and phosphorus, too, are required for bone growth and maintenance, and for maintenance of the composition of the body fluids. The thyroid gland requires iodine for the manufacture of its hormone, thyroxine; deficiency results in goitre, or in children cretinism. Lack of zinc results in retarded growth of children and lack of development of the testes; it is deficient in breast milk. Iron too is absent from milk; both this and copper are necessary for blood formation. Fluorine is necessary for tooth development.

One could continue through the elements; in greater or lesser amount, a living body requires a wide diversity of substances for its structure and

Table 4.7: Summary of Functions of Minerals and Manifestations of Mineral Deficiencies

Mineral	Function	Characteristics of the deficiency state
calcium	formation of bones and teeth	rickets
	regulation of muscle contraction, nerve	osteomalacia
	irritability and the rhythm of the heart-	osteoporosis
	beat activation of some enzymes	tetany
	blood clotting	
phosphorus	formation of bones and teeth	emaciation
	constituent of high-energy compounds,	fragile bones
	nucleoproteins, phospholipids, enzyme	rickets
	systems and buffer salts	
magnesium	activation of phosphates and oxidative	vasodilation
	phosphorylation enzymes	soft tissue
	relaxation of nerve impulses and muscle	calcification
	contraction	atherosclerosis
	a constituent of chlorophyll	tetany
sodium	regulation of pH, osmotic pressure and	nausea
	water balance	
	transmission of nerve impulses	anorexia
	active transport of glucose and amino	muscular weakness
	acids	and cramps
potassium	regulation of osmotic pressure and acid-	weakness, anorexia,
	base balance	abdominal distention
	activation of a number of intracellular	tachycardia
	enzymes	
	regulation of nerve and muscle irritability	pulmonary edema
		adrenal hypertrophy
chlorine	activation of amylase	poor growth in rats
	a constituent of hydrochloric acid	
	regulation of osmotic pressure and acid-	
	base balance	
sulphur	part of some amino acids, some vitamins,	not found
	some hormones, bile, melanin	
	synthesis of sulphomucopolysaccharides	
	detoxifying agents	
iron	part of haemoglobin, myoglobin and heme	anaemia
	enzymes	
copper	hemopoiesis, metabolism of vitamin C and	anaemia
	energy, formation of melanin, phospho-	depigmentation of hair
	lipids and elastin	(in animals)
		demyelination of nerve
		bone disorders

Source: Robson (1972).

function. Two problems arise: first, are these elements available? second, are they in balance with the calories present in the food? Will the necessary calorie intake provide enough of these important substances? In sedentary societies, probably in many cases the requisite calorie intake will be short of one or more essential elements; this leads to over-eating and obesity. In poorer communities dependent on a staple diet of starchy food, excess calories will not be consumed so that deficiency diseases appear. Either way, man is the victim of the ecological change to an agricultural life, which he himself has engineered. Today, these problems are better understood and foods are fortified so that calorie intake is better balanced with requirements of necessary food substances. The chemical structure of the vitamins is known and synthetic products are available at the chemists' shops. Nevertheless, much still remains to be learnt and we are still faced with the early onset of 'senescent' diseases in affluent societies, diseases probably associated more with inadequate feeding habits than with senescence.

Table 4.8: Changes in Food Consumption 1955-65, United States Households

| Food | Per cent change in household consumption from 1955 to 1965 | | | |
	North-east	North Central	South	West
	Increases			
Non-fat dry milk	140	100	138	129
Salad, cooking oils	92	100	117	19
Bakery products except bread	64	66	79	48
Beef	30	22	56	14
Chicken	20	27	21	37
Commercially frozen:				
Potatoes	150	375	1,300	250
Vegetables	30	21	62	25
Potato chips, sticks	140	60	83	46
Fresh fruit juice	381	267	167	575
Soft drinks	86	77	68	96
Fruit-made drink, punch, nectar	1,036	764	756	457
Peanut butter	50	57	67	45
	Decreases			
Fresh fluid milk	12	18	23	24
Evaporated milk	23	42	40	46
Butter	26	34	54	40
Shortening	30	35	37	49
Flour	31	31	50	42

| Food | Per cent change in household consumption from 1955 to 1965 | | | |
	North-east	North Central	South	West
		Decreases		
Sugar	7	20	15	22
Fresh white potatoes	18	18	15	25
Fresh vegetables	18	17	19	15
Fruit:				
Fresh	5	21	11	15
Commercially frozen	64	50	43	38

This table reveals changes in feeding habits in the United States between 1955 and 1965. The change from fresh foods to 'freezer' feeding is obvious. It is too early for assessments to be made of the significance to health of these radical changes, though the increase of enteric diseases is undoubtedly associated with it.

Source: Household Food Consumption Survey, Report No. 2, USDA, 1968.

5 NEW DISEASES

Shifting agriculture in time gave way to more settled agricultural methods. Irrigation, of itself, demanded settlement and more sophisticated farming implements. The digging stick gave way to the hoe, the spade and the plough. Farms appeared outside the irrigated areas, and the land was dug sufficiently deeply to make settled agriculture possible; the value of rotation, fallow and manure was learned. These developments inevitably led to the establishment of small agricultural communities living in villages, such as that at Jericho, perhaps not unlike native villages found today all over Africa and in many other parts of the world. Food was produced with less labour, leaving more time for leisure and leading to the creation of an artisan class, both for the production of essential tools and implements and also engaged in creative arts.

In the earlier years of the Neolithic Age, settlements such as these were unfortified, but in the later years they were all fortified, indicating that dangers had arisen from raiders intent on robbing the inhabitants of their property. By this time, wealth had considerably increased because of widespread trade, which was largely ship-borne. Amber and other trade goods, such as skins, were brought from Scandinavian countries to the Mediterranean both by sea route round the Bay of Biscay, and by the well-known 'Amber Route', which used the European river systems. Inevitably, villages were coalesced into towns, which could be enclosed in walls, and were more easily defensible. The foundation of towns and cities was of obvious benefit to trade and commerce, culture, the arts and science. It brought with it also the division of communities into rich and poor, jealousies and rivalries, a class system, civil servants and soldiers, lawyers and law-givers, rulers and ruled, and taxation to pay for it all. Indeed, it brought all the great benefits of which we complain today. Increased prosperity also brought a great increase of population living in towns at the expense of those living in rural areas.

These developments also brought the curse of the 'monoculture', which has been the bane of civilised peoples from the time when the first city was founded to the present day, the main weapon with which the environment has combated the attempts of man to battle with it. By an inevitable logic, the sophisticated and probably likeable primate, *Homo sapiens*, was driven by the urge to survive from being a hunter of animals and gleaner of natural produce, within a few thousand years, to a dweller in cities with far less likeable qualities; in an environment which he did not understand and which after another 7,000 years he is only now beginning to master, and in a way which in time bids fair to encompass his destruction. For the monoculture is not nature's way. Monocultures defy the ecological laws, which provide inbuilt methods of destruction, when any species becomes too numerous or too concentrated. Crops and animals become so and are then faced with destruction by pests and diseases; man exposed himself to the same fate, which would no doubt have come about more quickly and in a different way, had not marauding armies periodically attacked his cities and burnt them to the ground. In time, the first great global empire to bring stability, that of the Romans, perished because of the inescapable play of nature's laws. Man from about 500 AD until the fifteenth century reverted to mainly rural dwelling under the feudal system, but began to rebuild large cities following the plague pandemic known as the Black Death which for illogical reasons caused a reversion to city-dwelling.

The illogical reasons are: first, that plague is not in normal circumstances a disease of cities but a rural or sylvan disease; second, that it was ship-borne and as such one would have thought that it militated against commerce and would, therefore, have contributed to the decline of cities. Plague had been around for a very long time before the Black Death. It caused a major catastrophe during the reign of the Roman Emperor, Justinian, who held sway in Constantinople from AD 527 to 565. Since that time, there had been lesser and more localised outbreaks. However, in the middle of the fourteenth century plague swept over the civilised world like an avenging angel, reaching England in 1348, and killed some 50 per cent of the population. The people indeed regarded the plague as a visitation of the Almighty inflicted on them as a punishment for their sins, although some found it difficult to explain why the just and unjust were equally visited.

In those days, the great entrepôt centre for trade with the Far East was the Crimea. In some part of Siberia, the black rats (*Rattus norvegicus*) had become infected with plague as a result of being bitten by fleas from wild steppe rodents, such as voles. The rats began to die, and, as they do in such situations, they migrated, carrying their infected rat fleas with them. Plague raged through Far Eastern countries from China to the Caucasus, millions of persons died before the disease reached Europe at all. In the Crimea, rats embarked in the trade ships and so carried infection to European ports, such as Genoa and Marseilles. At each port, where the galleys called, foci of bubonic plague were created. Such foci had occurred before and indeed such exist in many

parts of the world today. As a result, a few cases of bubonic plague
occur in persons unfortunate enough to be bitten by rat fleas. These
outbreaks are not especially serious and are easily controlled. On this
occasion, as in the days of Justinian and at a later date in 1665, a new
factor entered the situation. The character of the disease changed; 'bubonic' plague was converted to 'pneumonic'. Whereas bubonic plague is
acquired as a result of a flea bite, the far more deadly pneumonic form
is transmitted from an infected person in exhaled air. It was this which
resulted in the rapidity of spread and the appalling mortality. The plague
radiated outwards from the ports, being spread in pandemic form,
especially to the populations of cities and towns. The number of cases
in the towns were highest, but even villages in rural areas were not
spared. Estimates vary as to the numbers who died; indeed, there is no
agreement as to the population numbers of countries such as England,
where no census had been taken since the Domesday Book in 1086. It
is believed that some 50 to 60 per cent of the entire population of
Europe perished.

It is, of course, evident that crowded conditions in ports and towns
contributed to the rapid and fatal spread of the disease. However, one
may enquire whether there existed special factors which contributed to
the change in character of the infecting agent, a bacterium known as
Pasteurella pestis. The danger that this could happen had existed through
the ages; why then did it happen at this particular time? On enquiry, we
find a time of deteriorating social conditions. The heyday of the Middle
Ages, the so-called Golden Middle Ages, had passed by, that time when
countries were prosperous and monarchs could afford the luxury of
Crusades to wrest the Holy Land from the hands of unbelievers. Following the era of prosperity, populations had outstripped resources. The
agricultural methods of the day were inadequate to provide food for all
the hungry mouths; there had been droughts and harvests had been lost;
people in some countries were even dying of hunger. Trade had declined
and there was unemployment in the towns and cities. In rural areas,
where the people were in thrall of one kind or another to the great
feudal lords whether as serfs or tenants paying in kind, there was under-
employment rather than unemployment, because the landlords could
not provide sufficient work to satisfy all the duties that were due to
them.

It is believed significant that the plague struck at a time when communities were in great distress, undernourished, and lacking in resistance. Conditions of distress had existed also at the time of the Great
Plague in the Emperor Justinian's time. The Eastern Empire, centred

on Constantinople, had been racked with wars; the Visigoths were
ravaging Germany, France and Spain; the Ostrogoths had occupied Italy;
the Vandals had conquered north Africa and required to be subdued.
The plague of 1665 came also at a time of poor social conditions. In
England, the great Elizabethan era had passed; the country had been
torn asunder by the Civil War and the Commonwealth. In its deadly
form, therefore, plague has always struck at times when communities
are in states of stress and their resistance is lowered. Though an ancient
disease, believed first described in biblical times, the pneumonic form
is a 'new' form of the disease, which appears under conditions of social
distress depending for its spread on crowded urban conditions. The term
'new' is used advisedly because, as we shall see, urban man is prey to
many 'new' diseases, which were unknown to him before he adopted an
urban way of life.

The writer has discussed at greater length the theme of the 'new' diseases of man in a work entitled *Zoonoses: the Origins and Ecology of
Human Disease.* This I believed to be original thinking, until I discovered
an important paper by the well-known Australian virologist, Frank
Fenner, entitled 'Disease and Social Change', which was published in an
Australian journal to which one does not have ready access in this
country. It was gratifying to find that my own deductions were in large
agreement with his. Fenner was puzzled at the properties of a number
of diseases from which urbanised man suffers; namely that in the first
place they are diseases only of man; in the second place, they are 'den-
sity dependent'. Such diseases attack the community in epidemic or pandemic form; they cause illness from which some die, but those that recover are immune to further attack. They must, therefore, become
extinct, unless the population is sufficiently large to provide enough
susceptible persons to maintain them. They could not have been perpetuated in communities of the size which existed before man became
urbanised. Yet, they attack man alone, no animal sources of infection
being incriminated. So, where did they come from? Their appearance is
clearly a function of the urbanised state, and they have plainly arisen as
a result of man's defiance of ecological laws in crowding himself into
cities against the dictates of nature, a result of human monoculture. Let
us consider first the situation with regard to influenza, which both illus-
trates the points that have been made and gives a clue to the ways in
which these events have happened.

Influenza is caused by one of the myxoviruses, a large group of viruses
which includes that of measles, fowl plague and other important diseases.
Of the true myxoviruses, which cause the influenzas, there are three

main groups, A, B and C. The three share group characters, which enable them to be classified together, but they are nevertheless distinct from each other and share no common antigens, so that immunity to a member of one group confers no immunity to a member of the others. It is worthy of remark also that none of the true influenzas is a disease of any primate other than man. We are concerned here only with groups A and B. Influenza caused by Group B myxovirus is a disease of man alone; no other animal is naturally infected by it. Its distribution is world-wide, except that small, isolated communities, such as that on the island of Tristan da Cunha, do not suffer from the disease—or any other forms of influenza—unless infection is introduced by a visiting ship. Group B influenza occurs in epidemic form every three or four years, when infection is mostly confined to young children who have not previously suffered from the disease and so have no immunity and to older people in whom immunity is fading. However, influenza viruses are versatile parasites, and can develop small changes of antigenic structure sufficient to defeat low levels of immunity acquired from former infection. This phenomenon is known as 'antigenic drift', and is not to be confused with 'antigenic shift', to be studied below, in which the entire antigenic structure is altered, leaving whole communities and populations without any defences at all. Antigenic shift never occurs with the Group B myxoviruses, so that the disease behaves in an orderly predictable kind of way, infecting the children and killing a few of the older people from pneumonia.

How B-type influenza appeared in the human race as one of its very own 'crowd' diseases is suggested by the ecology of the Group A myxoviruses. The world-wide pandemics and epidemics of influenza are all caused by the Group A viruses, which for the most part behave in the same predictable way as Group B. Susceptible members of communities are attacked, usually in the winter months, and the disease disappears. Some 30 to 40 per cent usually suffer from the disease in each epidemic, and it may reappear the following year or in three or four years' time, the antigenic properties of the virus being slightly altered by antigenic drift. Its appearance is always shown by an increased mortality of elderly people from pneumonia.

However, every ten to forty years there appears an entirely new form of the disease to which the entire population of the world is fully susceptible and a global pandemic results. The pandemics have been appearing regularly for a great many years and include the catastrophic 1918-19 outbreak of Spanish Flu, which killed many millions of people. Meanwhile, we are concerned to discover how this 'antigenic shift' occurs, and where the newer sub-types of A-type influenza come from. Unlike Group B myxoviruses, Group A can infect also pigs, horses and birds, though infection is not normally passed from man to pigs or horses or vice versa. The position with regard to birds will be studied after looking more closely at the antigenic mechanisms of the virus. Now, each myxovirus consists of a core and a coat. The core contains 'core antigens', which are common to all group A viruses and are of lesser importance in the creation of immunity. The coat contains two 'surface antigens', which are at the root of the trouble. The first of these is the H (haemagglutinin) antigen, which causes clumping (agglutination) of red blood cells; the second is the N (neuraminidase) antigen, neuraminidase being a specific protein enzyme which disintegrates mucin and thereby permits the virus to attack the underlying mucous membranes, thus causing infection. These viruses also possess a virulence factor, which determines whether they are infectious to man, pigs, horses or birds. Hitherto, some 13 H antigens have been discovered and 8 N antigens. The different sub-types of influenza A virus contain differing combinations of H and N antigens. Thus a newly appearing sub-type may possess both H and N antigens, to which a population has not previously been exposed, or it may have a new H antigen and an old N antigen, or an old H antigen and a new N antigen. Only one new antigen is necessary for a population to be completely susceptible, immunity to previous sub-types being unable to confer protection.

All the known H and N antigens have been found in birds, but in no other group of animals. Those found in human, porcine and equine influenzas are distinctive and not spread between them. It was thus supposed that other sub-types of human, equine, and porcine influenzas must somehow arise from birds by a recombination of the surface antigens and the virulence factor. How this could happen has been shown in recent years in experiments using both tissue cultures and live animals. Each myxovirus particle contains eight genes. When the cell nucleus is penetrated by the virus, the coat is shed and the eight genes separate, stimulating the host DNA to reproduce them. The daughter genes then come together again to form new virus particles, which acquire new coats and are shed to infect more cells. When two virus particles of different sub-types infect the same cell, the daughter genes may hybridise, so that the newly formed 'virions' (virus particles) may possess a human virulence factor but avian surface antigens; the new virion is known as a 'recombinant'. That such happens in nature has not so far been proved, but little doubt is felt that this is the mechanism by which antigenic shift occurs and that birds are in this way the source of pandemic subtypes of influenza viruses. Most pandemic strains have been traced to Far Eastern countries, China, Hong Kong and so on, where ducks and other poultry are kept in intimate contact with the people, so it can readily be seen how these recombinants could occur.

The influenza story has been ably told by W.I.B. Beveridge in his entertaining small book *Influenza: the Last Great Plague*. The story is of interest in our context, because it shows how the 'new', 'crowd' diseases of man could have arisen from animal sources and almost certainly did. However, what is true of influenza is not necessarily true of others. It is not possible in the space available to outline all those involved; they have been reviewed in some detail in this author's *Zoonoses: the Origin and Ecology of Human Disease*. We may, however, briefly review the position with two diseases, for both of which clues as to their origins are discernible. These are typhus and syphilis. Both are evidently 'new' diseases and both peculiar to the human species. Both have had profound influence on human history. Equally with influenza, the common cold, caused by Rhinoviruses, is a 'new' and peculiarly human form of respiratory infection.

Classical typhus is caused by a micro-organism *Rickettsia typhi*. It is transmitted by human head or body lice (*Pediculus humanus capitis* and *P.h. corporis*), but not by pubic lice (*Phthirus pubis*). These lice are peculiar to man and infect no other species of animals, even other primates. Typhus is a disease of dirt, formerly associated with gaols ('gaol fever') and armies when encamped in insanitary conditions. It has indeed wiped out whole armies and caused millions of deaths, especially in Russia after the revolution in 1917. It has in this way had an important influence on the course of history. It is of especial interest that the intermediate host, the louse, also becomes sick when infected and dies within a week or two. The infecting organism will infect no other animal than man. However, there is a related disease, known as 'murine typhus', of which the infectious agent, the rickettsia, is morphologically indistinguishable from that of classical typhus. This is endemic in wild house mice in certain parts of the world, particularly Mexico. It is transmitted to man by mouse fleas, and then passed from man to man by head and body lice, as with classical typhus. The organism is distinguished from that of classical typhus, because it can be transmitted back to mice whereas classical typhus cannot. Here, then, we have a classical case, in which the steps can be traced whereby a 'new' 'crowd' disease has become adapted to man as the sole host. The lethal effects of the organism on the transmitting agent, the louse, are most unusual and indicate poor adaptation of the rickettsia to the louse, a further indication of a 'new' association.

Syphilis is also a disease solely of man, and seemingly a 'new' disease, having possibly first appeared in the days of the ancient Greeks. It is venereal, being transmitted from person to person during the act of copulation, whether heterosexual or homosexual. It is caused by a spirochaete organism, known as *Treponema pallidum*. The evidence suggests that it originated in its present form at second-hand from the disease of yaws, prevalent in the wet tropics, or at third hand from a minor infection from which monkeys suffer in tropical Africa. The disease in the wet tropics, that of yaws, is transmitted from person to person by contact and causes severe lesions of the bones, such as 'sabre leg', which are readily identifiable in microscopic sections and distinguishable from those of other treponemal diseases. The distribution of this disease coincides to a great degree with the disease of wild monkeys which is so mild as to be only detectable with difficulty. There are transient skin lesions and enlarged regional lymph glands. This disease was discovered and described by the well-known French scientist, Andre Fribourg-Blanc. In the dry tropics of the north and south of the wet tropical zone, there exists another treponemal disease, known as 'treponarid' or 'endemic syphilis'. This is not venereal, but transmitted by bodily contact, as with yaws. This disease has a remarkable distribution, since it occurs along the migration route of aboriginal peoples from Africa to the Middle and Far East to China, and south through Indonesia, to Australasia and Australia itself, where the aborigines become infected. However, it is only found in peoples of aboriginal type, who have survived in pockets along this route. Like yaws this disease is identifiable and distinguishable by a study of microscopic sections of bone. Now, the treponematosis of more advanced peoples is the true venereal syphilis, so how and why did 'treponarid' or 'endemic syphilis' become converted into the dreaded venereal disease, which has so affected monarchs and leaders of men and led them into undesirable and irrational actions? The answer is simple. When men and women began to wear clothes, the condition for body to body contact, by which other treponematoses are spread, ceased to exist, except during copulation. The organism mutated and became adapted to transmission as a venereal disease.

Many other diseases of man can be quoted, which affect him alone and which have all the characteristics of 'new' diseases. Amongst the enteric diseases, one salmonella, that which causes typhoid fever (*Salmonella typhosum*) fits the definition; amongst the dysentery organisms, there is *Shigella dysenteriae*, which causes an acute and often fatal form of dysentery, and which affects man alone. Both with the salmonellas and the shigellas, there are numerous allied organisms with a greater host range, which are candidates for the ancestry of the purely human pathogens, developed without doubt during thousands of years of living in crowded and insanitary conditions. Man has acquired even his own species of tuberculosis, *Mycobacterium tuberculosis hominis*, and all know how great were the ravages of tuberculosis in crowded and insanitary towns and cities until a generation ago; indeed, they still are in many Far Eastern cities, where hygiene is unimproved. Tuberculosis is of especial interest, since it became of significance in the great conurbations, replacing leprosy. Leprosy is caused by an allied organism, *Mycobacterium leprae*, and there is a cross-immunity to a certain degree between the two diseases. Immunisation with the BCG tuberculosis vaccine gives a high degree of protection against leprosy also. Leprosy is a disease, slow of development. Infection is acquired as a result of long and intimate contact, as between a mother and her child. Crowded and insanitary conditions provided a better opportunity for the spread of tuberculosis at the expense of leprosy, so leprosy was crowded out and tuberculosis admitted to replace it. Tuberculosis resulting from the bovine strain of tubercle bacilli, *Mycobacterium tuberculosis bovis*, was present in Egypt in the times of the Pharaohs, as is evident from the existence of Potts' disease or tuberculosis of the spine. This form of tuberculosis is associated with the bovine strain, but not with the human. One may suppose, therefore, that the human strain was derived from the bovine.

The greatest killing disease of man world-wide is malaria, a disease which takes a terrible toll of life amongst children in tropical countries, and which, in many that survive, leaves mental impairment and inability to learn and be educated, possibly accounting in part for the backwardness of backward races. Here, too, a specially virulent representative of this family of parasites has become evolved from relatively innocuous ancestors; if not a 'new' disease in the strict sense of the word, at least a new variant.

The guessing game as to which diseases of man are 'new' or new variants of old diseases could continue indefinitely. Smallpox can definitely be included in this category. Can some of the cancers or such diseases as multiple disseminated sclerosis qualify? We shall not know, until the etiology has been discovered. The 'new' diseases are nature's response to the adoption of a new way of life, life in crowded conditions —monoculture. With some, a contributory factor has been the poor hygienic circumstances which have accompanied the crowded way of life, so ably described by Sir Cedric Stanton Hicks in an earlier volume of this series. Today, many of these diseases—most, I suppose—are controlled by drugs or antibiotics, or by vaccines, the incidence of others, such as cholera, has diminished since pure water supplies have been available and sewage has been disposed of in a safe manner. We should, however, take note of two conditions, which have worsened in recent times, wholly or in part because of improvements in the way of life. The first of these is poliomyelitis and the second enteric disease generally.

Poliomyelitis has, of course, today been virtually eliminated by the development of vaccines, just as tuberculosis has succumbed to drugs found to be effective against it. In the recent past, however, it accounted for a great many deaths, mostly of younger persons but also of young adults in the 25-35 age group, often mothers of young families. Perhaps, saddest of all was the prospect of promising young persons, crippled for life and unable to adopt careers appropriate to their ability. How much talent was lost through these tragic causes will never be known. In countries where hygiene is less strict, poliovirus, a member of the entero-virus group, is widespread and virtually all children become infected at a very young age as a result of faecal contamination of their food. In very young children up to the age of two years or so, infection with poliovirus is usually inapparent, though immunity to re-infection is induced. Death or disablement only occurs in children or adults protected from infection in their early years. Poliomyelitis tragedies were, therefore, a direct result of improvements in standards of hygiene, a somewhat anomalous back-handed swipe of the environment at those who defied the laws of ecology.

The only group of diseases which has been on the increase in recent times, is that of enteric infection resulting from consumption of contaminated foodstuffs. This again may appear at first sight surprising, when there are so many rules and regulations controlling food storage and preparation. Nevertheless, unsuspected dangers have appeared associated with newer ways of life in relation to food preparation and consumption. These dangers are associated with pre-packaging, deep-freezing and the keep-warm cabinet. Episodes involving hundreds of persons have occurred on long-distance flights, holiday cruises, and receptions and other social occasions. The deep-freeze preserves infection in contaminated food and the warm-up or keep-warm cabinet can act as an incubator, if the temperature falls below regulation levels, ensuring that after a few hours even one pathogenic organism has multiplied to billions. In the United States, there are regular reports of outbreaks of acute food poisoning, mostly associated with outdoor receptions, for which the food has been wholly or partially prepared a day or two before, stored in the refrigerator and then placed either in warming cab-inets or simply in the heat of the day. There are very few reports of trouble in connection with drug-stores or drive-in roadside kiosks, no doubt because food is normally cooked against each order, usually in sight of the customer. The British habit of the 'pub meal' fills one with horror. Sausages, pies, fish or chicken portions are placed early in the day in keep-warm cabinets and served to customers over a period of several hours.

The sources of contamination are mainly threefold: first, the original food may be infected; second, the original food may be contaminated by some person engaged in dressing and packaging it; third, infection may come from one of the kitchen staff engaged in the cooking and preparation of the food. In the first category, poultry is most often in-criminated, usually chickens or turkeys, though other meat products may also be to blame. Of course, all forms of meat are inspected and passed fit for human consumption, but infection may be inapparent and in any case an inspector watching thousands of birds passing at ten-second intervals on a conveyor belt for several hours faces an impossible task. Such cases are rarely detected until outbreaks of enteric disease have occurred and are traced back to their source. In the second event, a food dresser may harbour a salmonella infection, and with improper cooking and subsequent handling of the food even one organism can multiply to cause an outbreak of food poisoning in the way described. Kitchen staff may be responsible for causing contamination of food with salmonellae in the same way, but they provide additional dangers. A septic finger may introduce staphylococci, usually *S. aureus,* to the food and this organism causes severe and unpleasant intestinal symptoms. They can also introduce streptococci to the food, if suffering from a septic throat, and in this way cause an outbreak of streptococcal pharyn-gitis or laryngitis.

Infectious hepatitis also appears to be on the increase, the transmis-sion of which is associated with contamination of food and water with faeces. Uncharacteristically, the virus which causes it can survive for long periods in water and outbreaks have occurred in cases where water is drawn from surface wells. It can also survive in sea water and shell-fish become contaminated and transmit the disease.

There is little realisation of the profound effects on disease ecology that have resulted in man from urbanisation. Not only is man himself affected; so are his crops and his domestic animals. Crops can only be grown by the continued use of pesticides, animals by vaccination, treatment with expens-ive drugs and anthelmintics. The scene is artificial, of man's creation, and we shall proceed to study its further effects in other ways.

6 GLOOM AND DOOM

It was established in the first chapter that survival curves for human populations, prior to the present century, conformed very closely to those of wild animal populations. The influences controlling population numbers are, however, different as a result of man's changed ecological circumstances. Throughout the centuries, pre-existing diseases have become more serious because of crowded conditions of life, and new diseases have appeared which would be unable to survive except in certain minimal population densities. These diseases have operated in various ways and at various levels. As with wild populations, mortality in young persons to the age of seven years or thereabouts has been very high. One cause has been malnutrition; another endemic diseases, such as malaria, a third epidemic diseases, such as diphtheria, usually regarded as diseases of childhood.

Amongst young adults, mortality was formerly highest among women as a result of accidents and septic conditions associated with childbirth. Nevertheless, the over-all expectation of life was no more than 40 to 50 years and deaths from enteric and respiratory diseases were very high. Cholera, typhoid and paratyphoid were rife in the cities and pneumonia, from which most people would suffer at some time, would prove fatal in some half of persons attacked. Then there were the chronic diseases, such as tuberculosis, which took a steady toll of life. To cap it all, severe epidemics, such as smallpox, would appear at not infrequent intervals and kill a great many people.

In spite of this, there was a tendency for population increase, so that in time numbers outstripped food resources, especially after unfavourable seasons resulting in crop failures. Human population numbers did not explode and crash in a small number of years like those of lemmings and other wild animals. Nevertheless, it has been suggested that human population numbers have been subject to cyclic variations of a similar nature, but that the periodicity is some 300 to 400 years, the length of time obscuring the result. It is worth while to examine this proposition but without the expectation that the time interval will show great precision. This is attempted in Table 6.1.

Though, as said, precise correlations are hardly to be expected, some sort of rhythm is evident. Prosperity and ease of living are built up over a period of some hundreds of years until a point is reached when further

Table 6.1

2000	BC (late Neolithic). A period of great prosperity with widespread trade and expansion. The rise of the Minoan, Egyptian, and Aegean civilisations.
1400	BC Overthrow of the Minoan and Aegean civilisations. Invasion of Egypt by the Sea Peoples.
1000-900	BC Rise of Babylonian, Assyrian and Persian civilisations. Recovery of Egypt.
600	BC Overthrow of Assyria and Babylon. Alexander conquers and overthrows the Persian Empire. The world in chaos, leading to the rise of Greek civilisation.
200	BC Rise of Rome and overthrow of the Greek and Carthaginian empires.
0-400	AD Pax romana—great prosperity.
600-900	AD Overthrow of Rome and barbarian wars.
900-1300	AD During this period, the picture is obscured by the opening up of the New World, but in general it was a period of wars, civil wars and unrest. Slow recovery from the Black Death, a recurrence of plague in 1665.
1700-1900	AD Industrial revolution. Rise of science and medicine. Increasing prosperity.
1900-	AD Great prosperity and amelioration of living conditions but savage wars, and population increase threatens to outstrip food resources. Beginning of decline.

expansion cannot be sustained by the environment; then the 'crash' comes rather suddenly. The process closely resembles that associated with population 'explosion' and 'crash' in those wild species which show this phenomenon. The underlying symptoms of the crash are also similar. Populations become too great for resources; signs of stress and tension are evident; there develop fighting and unnatural behaviour patterns. Finally, diseases, which are normally not too serious, assume much greater significance and take a heavy toll of life. We shall study the natural factors which control population numbers in a later chapter, and attempt to see how these operate in human communities. Meanwhile, it is necessary to assess what effects the rise of medical science has had on the cyclic patterns revealed in man.

Assuming that the present cyclic era started, as suggested, around 1700 AD, then on the time-scale basis we should be enjoying an era of unprecedented prosperity leading to the crash in a hundred years' time or so. Signs of the impending crash should be evident, namely food and other resources should be becoming scarcer in relation to a much-increased population. The increased population should be showing signs of stress and unrest, and there should be increased competition for scarce resources, struggle, wars and fighting. Deaths from sickness and disease should be on the increase, with the danger hanging over our heads that some new pandemic will arise to kill off a large proportion of the world's population and consign us to the beginning of a new cycle.

Few will deny that this is a reasonably accurate account of the situation in the world today, as we see it. World population has risen alarmingly, and concern is felt that food, energy and some material resources will be inadequate within the hundred years postulated. Western countries enjoy an unprecedentedly high standard of living, attained largely by means of food imports and imports of fertiliser to sustain high agricultural yields. Attempts have been made to raise agricultural yields in developing countries by conservation of water resources and notably by the so-called Green Revolution, which depends on the introduction of new heavy-cropping varieties of food normally grown, sustained by the use of fertilisers in large quantities. The Green Revolution has been in large measure a failure, because those countries which have experimented with it have failed to produce the large quantities of fertiliser required and have not the means to acquire them from overseas. In many parts of the so-called Third World, there already exist hunger, malnutrition, especially amongst the children, and even frank starvation. While there is little deprivation in Western countries, favoured foods are becoming more expensive, so that many people are finding that they cannot afford them, and are forced to change their ways of life by consuming less or by finding alternatives. Furthermore, national incomes are tending to fall short of what is required to pay for imports of food, fertiliser and animal feedstuffs. The result is inflation, the printing of paper money, and a fall in the value of some national currencies. At the same time, those Third World countries, which have control of natural resources, understandably demand higher prices for their products so that their people too can share in the current prosperity era.

The food situation has been aggravated, and appears likely to become more so, by the misuse of agricultural land and by over-exploitation of natural resources. Let us examine first the situation with regard to agricultural land.

It is a mistake to suppose that troubles attendant on misuse of agricultural land are of recent origin. In an earlier volume in this series, Sir Cedric Stanton-Hicks has shown how the old lands of Tuscany and Latium were misused in Roman times at the behest of absentee landlords, so that not only are they still infertile, but resultant swamps are malarious and so unhealthy as to be still uninhabitable. The periodic floods, which threaten cities such as Florence, he attributes to removal of the forest cover from the hills, and destruction of the ancient Etruscan drainage system. In their heyday, the Romans were not concerned: their grain was shipped from north Africa, the granary of Rome, to the port of Ostia at the mouth of the Tiber. What has happened to Ostia? It has recently been rediscovered and partially excavated beneath 20 feet of debris and silt washed down the river from the once imperial city. What has happened to the north African grainlands from which Rome drew her wheat? Most of these rich lands will today grow nothing; they are desert. It is easy to say that the misuse and destruction of good agricultural land by past generations was due to ignorance: good farming practices had not been invented. As Hicks shows, this is untrue, because in Tuscany and Latium the land was well farmed. It was properly cultivated, the crops were rotated, the land was given adequate periods of fallow in which to recover, and fertility was restored by adding manure to the soil. Destruction of good farm land was due to reckless exploitation. Quite apart from the north African grainlands, there was in Roman times good pasture over much of the Sahara. Nomadic herdsmen moved their flocks over the grazing and hunted wild animals. Still, a layer of humus covers much of the desert surface. If water is provided—and this is abundant in underground lakes and rivers—the soil proves fertile and crops can be grown. This vast area, which was admittedly delicately poised, has been lost for productive purposes because of exploitation by over-grazing, especially by goats. The southern fringes are still encroaching in the Haute Volta, Chad and Sudan. Attempts at reclamation show by their success that the destruction of the terrain has been due to human activities and not to climatic changes, as is sometimes suggested. The most successful efforts at reclamation of desert land are those practised in Israel, where even unpromising areas such as the Negev are being restored to fertility. Conservation of the mountain heights has resulted in the reappearance of oaks and other trees which have survived in stunted form for two thousand years or more, and animals supposed extinct in these areas, such as the Asian Wolf (*Canis lupus pallipes*), have from some unknown focus reappeared.

What then was the fate of the old riverine agricultural systems, those of Egypt, Mesopotamia and the Indus Valley in Pakistan? They disappeared, except that of Egypt. The Egyptian agricultural system survived, because annually the soil was renewed by silt brought down by the Blue Nile from the mountains of Ethiopia. The irrigation systems of Mesopotamia have disappeared long since. In Pakistan, the formerly fertile province of Sind is desert and the ancient delta cities of Harappa and Kalibanga are surrounded by soils that can grow nothing. However in Pakistan Punjab, the land of five rivers, a fine irrigation system was built by British engineers in the nineteenth century. The rivers were dammed and irrigation canals were dug to convey the water in herring-bone fashion from river to river. This enterprise made of the Punjab a fertile garden, one of the largest irrigation systems in the world. By the mid-twentieth century, the system was showing signs of failure, and in response to an appeal by the late President Ayub Khan of Pakistan to President Kennedy in the United States, American specialists were sent to study the problem and found the solution; a solution, which was simple and probably could have saved the irrigation works of Mesopotamia, had ready advice been available. The irrigation canals, built by the British engineers, had been so successful that the water table under the land had risen significantly to within a few feet of the land surface. The water had brought dissolved salts to the surface, which contaminated the soil to such an extent that in some places nothing would grow in it. Such salt pans can be seen over extensive areas in Pakistan to this day, but the solution was simple and they are being effectively dispersed. Individual farmers were encouraged to rely less on canal water by introducing tube wells with pumps on their land. The irrigation water was thus taken from the water table, which became lowered and the salt deposits were washed back into the deeper layers of the soil. In this way, threatened land was saved, polluted land was reclaimed, and canal water became available to extend the irrigated area. Today, under excellent management of its irrigation systems, Pakistan has so far improved its agriculture as to be not only self-sufficient in wheat and rice, but also an exporter of food products.

One could continue the tale of devastated and ruined agricultural lands both in ancient and modern times. There have been over-grazing, over-cropping, sheet erosion and gulley erosion, wind erosion and dust bowls. Problems are today better understood; more enlightened steps are being taken to protect the land and reclaim it. However, let us now look at those influences which have become operative since the present era in the human cycle started around 1700.

It has been said that the opening up to agriculture of the Middle West of the United States in the nineteenth century was a major disaster for Britain. This coincided with the time when the Industrial Revolution was getting into its swing. For Britain, the Industrial Revolution brought a radical change of the whole social structure, which was only possible because of the availability of cheap imported food from the American continent. Rural areas were depopulated to provide labour for the factories. Towns unable to accommodate such big populations became squalid slums, and farmlands were enclosed for stock-raising in place of grain production. The diet of the people came to rely greatly on potatoes instead of the traditional foods of wheat flour and meat. The Industrial Revolution is regarded as having started around 1760, when James Watt succeeded in adapting steam engines to impart a rotary movement to machines. Before this, engines could only be used for vertical motion as in pumping water from mines. Now steam power could be adapted to the production of textiles with the result that cottage industries, such as spinning and weaving, were largely transferred to factories, causing great distress in country areas by taking away supplementary earnings from women and children essential to families for comfortable living. At the same time, there was a greatly increased demand for coal as a power source for the new technologies and for provision of coke for production of pig-iron. Transport systems also required to be improved; turnpike roads were built and a comprehensive canal system constructed. In industrial towns and cities, the air became so polluted by smoke and dust that they were in permanent gloom, summer and winter, and children, on an inadequate diet, suffered extensively from rickets. At the same time, the population grew and working conditions in the mines and factories were appalling.

In the midst of this distress, there arose a new millionaire class of coalmasters, ironmasters and industrial chiefs, who were hard-working but acquired great fortunes and were able to live the lives of princes, while neglecting their workpeople. Britain herself, in the forefront of the Industrial Revolution, acquired a position in the world of unprecedented wealth and influence and the greatest empire the world had ever seen. Up to the time of the First World War, nearly half of the world's land surface was coloured red on the maps. At the same time, research, science and the arts flourished, and outstanding progress was made in medicine and the biological and physical sciences. This was achieved at the expense of social instability, destruction of rural life, and a rift between rich and poor, which has not to this day been healed although the rich are no longer rich and the poor are no longer poor. Perhaps, most important of all, the country's population grew to a level at which it could not be fed from its own resources, rendering it especially vulnerable during two world wars and at times of economic depression, when difficulty is experienced in paying for essential imports.

In the United States, the effects of the Industrial Revolution in Britain were probably also in the long run unfavourable, although exports of grain, cotton and other products brought much-needed capital at a time when it was badly needed for the development of the country. The Midwest farmers became very rich and much farm land was misused, giving rise eventually to the Dust Bowl conditions of the 1930s. The country as a whole was able to develop a standard of living that was higher than that in any European country, and which it has been able to retain to this day. In the grainlands, this prosperity sowed the seeds of decline. Birth rates in rural areas were exceptionally high and population increased to too high a level. At the same time, new farming territories were developed in the British Dominions, notably Canada, and in South America, with the result that demand for agricultural products declined and great grain surpluses were created, the government eventually paying subsidies to farmers to leave land uncropped. The United States also developed a technical lead in manufacturing industry over other industrial countries, so that it became less reliant on the export of agricultural produce and could afford to overlook distress in rural areas.

Both the United States and Canada still produce grain surpluses, which are exported to stave off shortages in countries where there is insufficient. Such shortages are becoming increasingly numerous, occurring in Russia, China, and in other areas which have few resources with which to pay for them. Such salvage operations provide no long-term solution, so long as world population continues to rise. The world food situation thus supports the supposition that the human 300 to 400-year cycle still operates. However, the maintenance of the present system, developed as a result of the Industrial Revolution, demands more and more power and energy to sustain it, and we may now examine the situation in relation to energy sources.

Until 250 years ago, man's use of energy was confined to man and woman power, animal power, and the use of natural energy resources, such as wind and water. Energy in the form of fire, also derived mostly from burning natural resources such as wood and peat, was used for heating and cooking. By an ingenious compound of chemicals to make gunpowder, energy was used in the form of guns to destroy man's fellow men and their works, and to kill animals for food. Coal had been mined since Roman times, and was used for heating and for the smelting of iron and other metal ores. Fire had been known and used from time immemorial. Engines of one kind or another, of a crude or sophisticated type, had been constructed in the form of wind or water mills for a variety of purposes, including land drainage as in the East Anglian fenland of England or for raising water for irrigation as in Egypt and Mesopotamia.

Only eighteen thousand years ago, an infinitesimal period in race history, the northern races of man were living adequate lives in arctic tundra with no other form of energy than fire by which to warm themselves and cook. The lives of their descendants today come virtually to a halt if the electric power fails, so dependent is Western man on his power sources.

If the clock were put back, one wonders how many of those living today could survive in the arctic conditions in which his ancestors were reared? Few, one supposes, of those who drive around in the company's Rolls-Royce. And yet, such a situation might easily occur. There are many theories, but profound ignorance as to the causes and periodicity of ice ages. One thing is known—that they occur and recede with great momentum once a new cycle has started. Another thing is known, that in 250 years of luxurious living man has virtually exhausted the world's stocks of fossil fuel; coal stocks may last another 200 to 300 years, oil stocks 100 years at most. The combination of a new ice age with exhaustion of energy resources could easily take man back to where he started eighteen thousand years ago, within a few hundred years. The dangers are realised by most people, but not to the extent of the catastrophe that would occur in such a situation. The final tragedy would undoubtedly be heralded by internecine struggles between peoples for the diminishing energy resources, struggles in which one opponent or another would inevitably set off a nuclear bomb, thus at least solving the population problem, possibly for ever. Scientists today are feverishly, if belatedly, seeking for new sources of energy, while lip-service is paid to the conservation of existing energy sources. One need feel little doubt that adequate new sources of energy will be found in time, but time is short and it could well be a photo-finish. One can only urge that the solution may be found, not in rivalry and struggle, but in sensible co-operation between power blocs and peoples.

As our 300 to 400-year cycle draws to an end, the crash could come equally well from climatic change or exhaustion of energy sources or a combination of the two. Other possible causes of doom are also predicted. One such is that man, living on his own dung—and chemical—hill will destroy himself by pollution. This theme will not be pursued here. The dangers are real, but authorities are reacting sensibly to pressure by environment groups in all advanced countries, and efforts to overcome the dangers are likely to be successful. There is far less realisation that, apart from energy sources, man is using other natural resources, which are important if not vital to his civilisation, at a rate which threatens their early depletion. Synthetic materials are mostly made from coal and oil, so that when they are exhausted the synthetics will disappear also. When the price of crude oil was drastically increased by the oil-exporting countries (OPEC), the cost of plastics was drastically increased also, proving the point. The figures in Table 6.2 show the estimated times before reserves of key materials are exhausted, allowing for: (i) increase of population at the present rate; (ii) a continuing rise in demand at the present level; and (iii) exploitation of possible new reserves or creation of new resources by innovation.

Table 6.2

Product	Estimated date of exhaustion
Iron and Iron-Alloy Metals	
Iron	2500
Manganese	2100
Chromium	2500
Nickel	2100
Molybdenum	2100
Tungsten	2000
Cobalt	2100
Non-Ferrous Metals	
Copper	2000
Lead	1990
Zinc	1990
Tin	1990
Aluminium	2100
Precious Metals	
Gold	1990
Silver	1990
Platinum	1990

Source: Ehrlich *et al.* (1971).

The estimates take no account of two important products, namely mercury and uranium. Mercury is fast approaching exhaustion already. Uranium supplies are limited, but their lifetime could be prolonged if fast-breeder reactors can be satisfactorily developed as a power source. The figures speak for themselves. Unless these approaching shortages can somehow be overcome, perhaps by supplies from extraterrestrial sources, civilisation as we know it is limited to a few hundred years. Man's ingenuity and inventiveness will, one is confident, overcome these difficulties, but it must be realised that the problem is with us now, and time is short. Together with failure of food and energy supplies, that of raw materials could of its own or in combination with other factors cause the collapse of our civilisation.

It will be evident that these dangers are largely a function of population size. Earlier recessions in human advance have been associated with population increases to levels that outstrip material resources. The position has been corrected when natural catastrophes, notably pandemic diseases, have resulted in drastically reduced population numbers. There are slight, but hopeful, signs that this drastic remedy might be avoided in the future. Advances in medical science and care during the past hundred years have had a twofold effect. In the first place, the expected life span in advanced countries has been improved from a variably low level to 70 years and upwards, and in backward countries the appalling toll taken by endemic and epidemic diseases has been controlled. In both cases, the result has been an alarming increase in population numbers, that increase which threatens the world's resources of food, energy and natural resources. On the other hand and in the second place, as people become more prosperous and live longer, there is a natural desire for more of the material comforts of life and to provide for a comfortable old age; large families are expensive, and there is a natural clash between the desire for a large family and that for material comforts for the parents and advantages also for the younger generation. In this clash, parents of their own accord limit families to numbers they can support in the life-style they desire. In Western countries and amongst the more affluent citizens of less affluent countries, family numbers have been progressively reduced over the last hundred years, and it could well be that the population problem will in time—in sufficient time one hopes—solve itself. The philosophy that unlimited aid is available to support innumerable children of inadequate persons, of course, defeats this natural process. It would appear preferable to promote prosperity amongst all the persons of a state and of all states, within differing standards of luxury; then the population problem could disappear of its own accord. Persons living in poverty have naturally little regard for the future, and it would appear to be a more logical approach to the situation, and ecologically sound, to provide them with incentives to care for the future, rather than to embark on programmes of compulsory sterilisation, which can only be self-defeating.

The increased expectation of life in advanced communities has been achieved by improvements in the standards of living, including control of hygiene, and by the development of drugs and vaccines, by which infectious diseases can be controlled or treated. There are other categories of disease, which medical science has so far failed to fathom and cannot control. Many deaths still occur from these from childhood to old age.

These are the cardio-vascular and cerebro-vascular diseases, diseases of the kidneys and other organs, genetical diseases and mental ill-health, to mention a few. We shall be studying some of these in succeeding chapters, and we shall find evidence that some at least are associated with crowded urban living in an ecological environment that is unnatural to man and to which he is only slowly becoming adapted. However, our present quest is to see whether dangers still exist that some uncontrollable epidemic could arise, in which a sizeable proportion of mankind would perish. The answer must unhesitatingly be that dangers do exist of such an occurrence, which medical science would be totally unable to control in sufficient time. The influenza viruses are one possible source of such an infection, and I shall quote the last paragraph of W.I.B. Beveridge's *Influenza: the Last Great Plague.* Beveridge is an acknowledged world expert on virus diseases of animals, and a consultant to the World Health Organization:

> Parasites prosper when their hosts become numerous and crowded. The human race has become very numerous and crowded. Huge aggregations of people and a vast air transport system have provided ideal conditions for the spread of the airborne parasite we are concerned with. Influenza pandemics could well become increasingly serious, and there is no known reason why there should not be another catastrophe, one like that of 1918, or even worse. The disease known as fowl plague, due to an influenza virus, causes practically 100% mortality in chickens. Influenza is no respector of national or climatic barriers and affects rich and poor countries alike. It is a global plague: a spark in a remote corner of the world could start a fire that scorches us all.

The versatility of viruses, by which they can mutate and recombine, spells danger. It is not only the myxoviruses of influenza that pose the threat; there are thousands of viruses which could produce a new and fatal variant. However, we have seen above that this does not happen under normal circumstances, only when populations increase to such an extent that the quality of life has first deteriorated to a drastic extent. To avoid these dangers, medical science cannot be expected to do the impossible; it is for man himself to contrive for the preservation of the habitat and so of his own health.

I shall no doubt be criticised by reviewers, because I have called this chapter 'Gloom and Doom'. Here is another writer, it will be said, who attempts to make our flesh creep with tales of the wrath to come. One reviewer, in the *Church Times* of all journals, said this of my earlier volume in this series, *Ecology and Earth History*, which said the exact opposite, and which he had obviously reviewed without reading. I see no reason why the human race should crash like the lemmings, though the evidence suggests that the prosperity cycle is ending with the 300 to 400-year cycle. Undeniably, there are difficult years ahead, while man solves his problems; if these should lead to armed struggle between nations and power blocs, a crash could well occur, the effects of which would last for centuries. If people can co-operate, no doubt the years of decline can be avoided or ameliorated, giving rise to a new cycle of advance and prosperity. To see problems in advance and face them squarely is not to label oneself a prophet of doom and gloom; only in this way can we tackle these problems. Like the Roundheads in the Civil War, we must put our trust in God, but keep our powder dry. God will not help those, like my *Church Times* reviewer, who will not by their own efforts look to the future.

In the chapters that follow, we shall study those diseases that most beset urbanised man, and which have replaced infectious diseases as the major cause of death. First, in the next chapter we shall examine what is known of the condition of 'stress', a reaction both of wild populations and of man to crowded living. Stress is an important factor in the etiology or severity of many diseases, both infectious and non-infectious, and underlies many of the tensions responsible for unrest, social violence, racial intolerance and wars between nations. Only in recent years has a beginning been made to study the underlying physiological causes.

Nature's economy, before the arrival of agricultural man on earth had, over the millennia during which life had existed, become fairly adjusted both between different life forms and between life forms and the environment. The population numbers of any one species were never permitted, more than temporarily, to become too numerous for the resources of the habitat. The basic concept is one of great simplicity, but one that humankind today rejects. More young, whether animals, plants or other forms of life, are produced than can be expected to survive. Nature's problem is, therefore, to remove the surplus and so regulate numbers. Harsh as is this law of nature, the results are beneficial. The surplus that are removed are those less fitted to survive; one carefully avoids the term usually used, namely the weakest, for the following reasons.

Conditions in an ecosphere are constantly variable as regards climate, food availability, camouflage requirements for protection, and places in which to rear the young. Therefore, those members of a community most fitted to survive in one generation may differ from those most fitted to survive in succeeding generations. Of course, those individuals that are weakest because of inborn genetic or congenital defects are the first to suffer extinction, and this is beneficial to the community as a whole. Nevertheless, a far more subtle method of quality control is exercised, known as the 'polymorphic genetical system'. All life forms resulting from sexual methods of reproduction are hybrids, in the sense that their genes are composed of one factor obtained from the male parent and one from the female. Where these two factors are identical, they are 'homozygous' for that factor; where the genes from the two parents are different, they are 'heterozygous'. The genes are shuffled around in succeeding generations, giving an enormously variable combination of characters that are possible in response to changing circumstances. In one generation, possibly a light colouration is advantageous; in succeeding generations a dark colouration may have greater survival value. In a surprisingly short time, light-coloured specimens mostly or entirely disappear, and all are dark. Such changes regularly recur in certain species of moths. Moths in sooty towns, where the tree barks are blackened, become dark, whereas their country cousins are light. However, the capacity to revert to a light colour is retained because of the polymorphic genetical system; the genes for light colour are retained in the heterozygous cells, though not in those that are homozygous for dark colour. Light colour can quickly re-appear, when two genes for light colour come together during mating. This is, of course, a great simplification of the system, since colour is determined by a number of genes in a complex manner, and this gives even greater flexibility to the system.

Populations also regulate their own numbers by inborn behaviour patterns. The most important are the territorial and hierarchy systems, which operate together. All vertebrates, at any rate, which live in social communities observe a hierarchy with dominants and subordinates. The ways in which the dominants and subordinates are selected in different species has been much studied and can be somewhat complicated. It is variable in different groups of animals, and varies with the way of life. In some, such as stags and horses, the males fight for the females. The fighting resembles the set-piece battles of medieval warfare. It is rarely to the death, since the loser usually admits defeat and retires from the scene to live a solitary existence, perhaps to try again with another male or in another year when he has grown stronger and his former antagonist older and weaker. In other animals, such as birds, selection of the male by the female follows an elaborate courtship procedure, when he displays the beauty of his feathers. In either case, neither males nor females will mate and produce young unless they can acquire a 'territory'. A territory must be an area of the habitat of sufficient size to provide enough food for the family, concealment against predators, and a suitable place in which to rear the young. Once a territory has been acquired, this is carefully marked; mammals mostly ring it with scent markers; birds on the other hand proclaim it in their song. Such territories are respected and virtually never invaded by other members of the same species. Even a stronger animal, caught trespassing on another's territory, will shrink away when challenged, except perhaps in the rutting season when a strange male may challenge the existing herd male both for his females and his territory, since both go together. This very remarkable and gentlemanly behaviour came into being tens of millions of years ago, and operates in animals so far removed as sticklebacks and lions. It promotes order, stability and survival. It also ensures that surplus animals are available, either when population numbers have been reduced because of unfavourable conditions or some catastrophe, or when, because of favourable conditions, the species is able to spread beyond its former limits. That man himself conformed to these laws of nature in pre-agricultural days may be accepted as a certainty and is attested by studies such as those of van der Post on the Bushmen peoples of the Kalahari.

We are presently concerned with the fate of the subordinates, those that do not acquire a territory or a female—or if they acquire a female, do not have the right to breed because they have no territory. This again varies with the innate behavioural patterns of the species to which they belong. In some species, they remain with the community for which they perform needful services, though debarred from the delights of reproduction. In others, they are driven out; in this case, they are likely to fall victims to predators, unless nature has proved bountiful and they can open up new territories. Most bizarre of all is the behaviour of chimpanzees. When the females come on heat, as they do in a monthly rhythm as with human beings, the old man of the troop will copulate until he is sated, and then the younger subordinate members are also accepted by the female and they also copulate with her. With wolves, in which the females come on heat for a limited period once a year only, there may be unmated males and females in the pack, but there is no mating except between the dominant male and female. Only when one or other dies or is killed will he or she be replaced. All the same, an un-mated male will make a beeline for a husky bitch on heat kept out by the owners to mate with a wolf. Unmated males will also travel great distances in search of suitable new areas in which to establish a territory; if found, they will bring their own females and establish a new pack.

In spite of these excellent regulations, conditions of over-population do frequently occur, either because excess young have not been elimin-ated in one way or another, or because drought or famine has reduced the size of the territorial areas. In such cases, there occurs a remarkable series of events, which are known, for want of a better term, as 'stress'. It is this which we need to study in relation to man's newer condition of life resulting from urbanisation and post-agricultural ecology.

There can be few people in highly cultured Western societies who do not at least from time to time suffer from feelings of anxiety, tension, irritability, inadequacy or stress. So we all know what stress means, or at least what it does to us. In some ways, stress may be a pleasurable thing, as in anticipation of a performance on the stage, a date with a beautiful girl, or riding in a race. On the other hand, the worries of modern life can induce a different kind of stress, which may be at the root of many of the diseases and ailments which beset us in our crowded way of living. It will help, therefore, to understand the roots, origins and mechanisms of these conditions, which are physiologically deep-rooted and not merely a mental state. Stress, under the same term, has been independently investigated by scientists studying the basic conditions of human ailments. It is today realised that both have been studying the same phenomenon, though in wildlife the condition is normal and physiological but in human beings largely pathological.

Stress, so far from being a psychological state as might be thought, depends on definable changes to the physiological status of the body. The organs primarily involved are certain glands of the endocrine system, of which the adrenal glands are the most important. These glands, as the name implies, lie adjacent to the kidneys. They consist of two portions, which become associated during embryonic life. The outer portion is known as the cortex and the inner as the medulla. The cortex is developed from the coelomic ridge of the embryo together with the sex glands— ovaries or testes. The medulla has an entirely different origin as an off-shoot of the sympathetic nervous system. The medulla is responsible for the production of adrenaline. The cortex on the other hand produces a range of specialised hormones known as cortico-steroids, which are of two groups, anabolic and catabolic. These hormones control metabolism, the catabolic steroids promoting a run-down of metabolism; the anabolic, a building up. Anabolic steroids have been used in athletes to promote muscular development and performance, though their use is now prohibited for this purpose. The cortico-steroids are essential to life; if they are cut off, as occurs in the acute stage of stress, the animal dies within minutes. One of the cortical hormones, cortisone, is widely used in medical practice as an anti-inflammatory agent.

The cortico-steroids are one part of a complicated biochemical mechanism which is not yet fully known. The adrenal cortex is very rich in essential fatty acids (EFA), of which some account has been given in an earlier chapter. Steroids are fatty substances and undoubtedly EFA are important to their manufacture. EFA cannot be utilised by the body in the absence of the fat-soluble vitamin E (alpha-tocopherol) and this vitamin is ineffective if there is a deficiency of the metal selenium. The adrenal cortex is also very rich in vitamin C (ascorbic acid). Vitamin E is an oil-soluble anti-oxidant. In the absence of anti-oxidants, EFA becomes oxidised to produce unpleasant toxic substances, so we may assume that this portion of the adrenal gland is equipped to handle EFA and manufacture from them the hormones so essential to life. The adreno-cortical hormones are in a sense antagonistic to those of the sex glands. Both are controlled by hormones from the pituitary gland, situated at the base of the brain. This gland produces a hormone known as adreno-cortico-tropic hormone (ACTH), which directs the output of cortico-steroids. If there is a high requirement for cortical hormones, the pituitary produces more ACTH, but at the expense of other hormones which

activate the sex glands. In conditions of stress, there is a high requirement of cortical hormones; consequently, the sex glands become less
active. The result is that in conditions of stress animals become less
fertile, less fecund, and tend to abort or resorb foetuses from the uterus.
Thus, in stressed conditions fewer young are born and this leads to population reduction. The pituitary itself is linked to a certain section of
the brain, the hypothalamus, and is thus itself commanded by external
stimuli arising from unfavourable physical or emotional conditions. The
stressed animal, when it dies, is easily recognised because the adrenal
glands, under pressure, are found to be much enlarged and the cells are
full of yellowish fatty substances. In the extreme situation, death may
occur from adrenal exhaustion, in which case the glands are shrunken
and flabby, containing neither hormone nor its precursors.

A stress situation can act either on an individual or on the community
as a whole. It has been found that subordinate members of a community
have enlarged adrenal glands as compared with the dominants, indicating
that they are stressed in the sense of requiring a greater output of cort-
icosteroid hormones; their inclination to mate will be correspondingly
reduced. If, on the other hand, an animal finds itself in a situation of
danger, initially the medullary portion of the adrenal gland takes over.
There is stimulation of the sympathetic nervous system and an outpour-
ing of adrenaline, by which the body and the senses are placed on the
alert and prepared for flight and fight. So long as escape is possible, the
animal remains keyed up and ready to preserve its life. If escape becomes
impossible, then adrenal medullary control is relaxed and demand for
hormones is switched to the adrenal cortex. Usually, in the case of an
animal doomed to succumb to a predator, the adrenal becomes quickly
exhausted and death occurs in the first stage of stress, that is from shock.
The rabbit captured by a stoat mercifully dies quickly from this cause,
as does the zebra which has fallen prey to lions or hunting dogs. Wild
animals that have been caged frequently pass into the second stage of
stress in which the adrenals become enlarged to compensate. If a second
cause of stress is superimposed on the original stress of capture and cag-
ing, the adrenals may again prove inadequate and the animal may die.
The second stressing event, which causes this, is often seemingly trivial.
Removal from a cage or den to better quarters is sufficient; the animal
has become accustomed to its surroundings which give it some sense of
security, and interference causes alarm. Some animals withstand stressing
situations better than others; some are notoriously susceptible and a
headache to animal importers and zoo officials. It might be thought that
stress was an attribute of higher animal forms with more developed and

sensitive nervous systems. This is, however, not the case. Snakes, for example, often refuse to feed after capture and eventually starve to death. I have known cases in frogs, where one of a pair dies and the mate remains in the water until it eventually dies of drowning. Some birds, of which geese are an example, will refuse to feed if a mate dies and succumb to starvation. Thus stress is a primitive physiological mechanism operative at all levels of vertebrate evolution.

It follows that there are few communities among social animals in which some members are not stressed to a greater or lesser degree, even if those affected are only the ones at the lower end of the pecking order. Diseased or injured animals become stressed as an automatic response to their disability. The seriously sick or injured animal seeks a place of concealment, where it can lie undisturbed. There it remains in a state of torpor until it dies or recovers. If disturbed, it shows aggression; if food is available, it will take some. Nature thus decrees a response to sickness or injury which gives the best chance of recovery. The stressed animal, on the other hand, has less ability to avoid predators and diminished resistance to infection. In entire communities, stressed states develop when the ecological balance is upset, either because the population has increased too much, or because climatic change or other influences have disturbed the habitat. The whole community then comes into a state of nervousness and tension. Members fight and some are killed; the young tend to be killed, and, in the case of carnivores and rodents, are eaten. The females mate less readily and do not become pregnant, they readily abort their foetuses or, as with some animals such as rabbits, the foetuses die and are resorbed in the uterus. Litter sizes of those foetuses that come to term are smaller than when conditions are more normal. At the same time, disease resistance is reduced and latent infections become active, causing deaths. Commensal organisms, which are normally harmless, become more virulent and cause epidemics. In these ways, the population again becomes adjusted to the habitat, and the state of stress disappears amongst the survivors.

Stress, then, is a remarkable and primitive neuro-endocrine mechanism, which promotes adjustment of animal communities with their environment and long-term survival of the species. By ensuring the removal of those members less fitted to survive, it enhances the genetic performance of the community and ensures the best possible adaptation to prevailing conditions acting through the polymorphic genetical system described above. The physiological mechanisms involved are little known. This author, as a result of long researches over some fifteen years, believes stress to be a form of chronic hypotension, the opposite of hypertension from which so many people suffer in the modern world. There appears to be an impairment of the blood flow through the great veins on its return to the heart for recirculation. It has been pointed out by myself and my collaborators that the abdominal section of the posterior vena cava is complex both in its structure and in its relation to other organs, such as the diaphragm, liver and kidneys. We have shown that blood return to the heart is impaired if the unusual form of muscle in this vein is thrown out of tone, and we believe that this is what happens in the stressed state. Under the strain of modern living, many people suffer from hypertension, and it is probable that a chronic hypotensive state may also exist.

Urbanised man, as is clear from what has already been said, is living in a highly unnatural habitat of his own making. His population densities are unnaturally high, and the natural laws of hierarchy and territory have been perverted. The dominants in human society are those with a natural talent for acquiring wealth, power or property, and not necessarily those best fitted to survive in a harsh environment. Territory is measured in terms of wealth rather than a niche in which to rear the young. Indeed, those who dominate the scene tend of their own choice to produce fewer young than their less fortunate kinsmen. Until recent times, the balance has been redressed by a high mortality from infectious disease, operative to a greater extent amongst the poorer sections of the community. At the same time, the natural laws, by which a neighbour's territory is respected, have been flagrantly flouted and tens of millions of persons have died in aggressive and disastrous wars of conquest. A balance of nuclear power has hopefully made global wars a thing of the past, and the more lethal infectious diseases have been controlled. Meanwhile, medical science is ensuring the survival of the weak and even of many of the genetically unfit. What then of the future, when longevity increases, populations rise, and natural controlling mechanisms are side-stepped? There is indeed abundant evidence that stress operates in human communities, both at individual and community levels. Heightened rivalries between persons and aggression between classes and nations are of themselves indicators of a state of stress both in persons and peoples.

It is not for this work to enter into sociological controversies. It may, however, be reasonably suggested that signs of unease due to community stress both exist and are becoming intensified. In an era of unprecedented luxury, affluence and social welfare, never were people more discontented This discontent is shown in rising crime rates, hooliganism, violence, class and racial struggles, terrorism and lawlessness, and rivalry on an international scale between different political creeds. All the signs are of community stress, which, as shown, may well lead to the point of explosion by the end of the 300 to 400-year expansion period. However, let us assume that man's superior intelligence will triumph and enable him to overcome the threatened storm, and study those ways in which stress is operating today on human health and happiness.

In its acute form, stress is known as 'shock', and is exemplified by the sudden death of the rabbit attacked by the stoat. As with all forms of stress, the causes may be psychological, as in the case of the rabbit, or physical. Physical causes are usually serious injuries, such as those resulting from a car accident or extensive burns. Such injuries are common enough in modern life. The cause of shock is well established to be a sudden hypotension with a steep fall of the blood pressure; blood accumulates in the veins and smaller blood vessels, and death occurs from failure of blood return to the heart with consequent heart failure. Apart from the acute form there are three stages to the stress syndrome. In stage 1, the resources of the adrenal glands are taxed to respond to some 'stressor' influence; if they cannot meet the demand, death occurs from shock. In stage 2, the adrenal becomes enlarged in response to the stressor influence; in this case, the animal is apparently normal, but is still chronically stressed and therefore in a state of tension and vulnerable. Stage 3 is the stage of exhaustion; this occurs when an animal in stage 2 stress is exposed to additional stressor influences, either by intensification of the pre-existing stress or by the appearance of a new stressor factor. A great many people living in crowded urban conditions are undoubtedly exposed to stressing situations, which would not be tolerable by the wildlife communities we have been studying in these chapters. It would not be surprising if they were in stage 2 stress with their adrenal glands compensated. Such a situation could account for lawlessness and aggression amongst some members of society, and on the other hand of feelings of inadequacy and symptoms of withdrawal amongst persons lacking aggressive instincts.

That a widespread chronic stress situation exists amongst a large section of urban populations is suggested by the numbers of persons who at some time in their lives suffer from neurological disturbances, and others who suffer from long-term or permanent mental derangement. A large proportion of available hospital space in a country such as Britain is occupied by mentally disturbed persons; some of them suffering from genetically determined mental diseases; many others in a state of 'withdrawal' from an environment with which they cannot cope. It may be suggested that unsocial habits, such as alcoholism and drug addiction, are also, in part at any rate, developed as a response to chronic stress and environmental withdrawal.

Stress also operates on another section of the community, the square pegs in round holes. Different people have varying capacities for different types of employment. Some are born to be leaders and become masters of empires or captains of industry; others are adapted to manual or literary skills and prefer to be directed in their activities. The natural leader will be unhappy and inefficient in a position where he cannot employ his talents, and become stressed. Conversely, the person who would be happy doing a routine and rewarding job, will be unhappy and inefficient if elevated to a position of responsibility; he too will be stressed. Furthermore, the ambitious man, or the man pushed by an ambitious wife, who fails to attain seniority will feel a sense of frustration and will also be stressed. It is such persons who succumb to serious episodes, such as strokes or coronary heart disease. The man who is successful and builds a great commercial empire is rarely troubled by these conditions; the man who succumbs is he who sets himself on such a course and fails. Another class of persons to become stressed in modern life are those who, though they may enjoy their employment, are exposed to exacting conditions, which demand continual and unremitting attention. The average car-driver is in some sense stressed, and it has been found that London bus-drivers suffer a higher incidence of coronary heart disease than bus-conductors.

Stress, then, is a basic foundation for some forms of mental disease and for episodes involving the circulatory system, such as stroke and coronary heart disease. The latter will be considered in more detail in a later chapter, in which it will be shown that stress has a direct effect both on the health of the arteries and on the clotting mechanisms of the blood. Stress undoubtedly profoundly affects a wide range of bodily functions, many of which have yet to be determined. Amongst other important functions to be affected is that of the immune mechanisms, so that stressed persons are more susceptible to infectious disease. Since immune mechanisms play some part in the development of resistance to cancer—or to the organisms which cause it, since cancer may prove to be a form of infectious disease—this may explain why stressed persons suffer more commonly than others; it is a saying amongst doctors that happy persons do not suffer from cancer. In populations of wild-living animals, the function of the stress phenomenon, as we have seen, is twofold: first, it matches population numbers to the environment; second, it promotes the survival of the best adapted. In pre-agricultural man, it undoubtedly had a similar effect. In spite of the rise of human populations in many parts of the world to undesirable levels, the effect may still have been important in rendering the stressed members of populations more susceptible to infectious diseases, which were the main population-limiting factors. In spite of such limiting factors populations did rise to levels that were too high, leading to the explosion and crash situation every three to four hundred years. In this too, we can find parallels in wildlife ecology. Man resembles in his behaviour that of exotic species introduced to a new environment, which is what indeed man is. The most obvious parallel is that of rabbits introduced to Australia, where there was a suitable habitat and no predator, once man virtually extinguished the dingoes. The rabbits multiplied to such an extent that they were destroying the habitat on which they lived. This they continued to do until man introduced a new controlling factor in the disease myxomatosis. The disease, at first of great virulence causing a mortality of 98 per cent, in time came into balance with the rabbits, controlling their numbers but permitting their survival. A similar situation exists with elephants in Africa. Elephants were formerly at liberty to roam widely and seasonally, following their elephant trails for long distances to places where food was abundant. In present years, they have been confined to game reserves, where their numbers have come to exceed the carrying capacity of the land. As a result, the habitat has been largely altered; the tree cover has disappeared, and the elephants have to survive on an unnatural diet of coarse grass which has replaced the trees. The breeding potential of the elephants has diminished, but their numbers remain too great. Signs of stress are evident in the elephants, as we shall see in a later chapter.

Medical statistics have radically altered since the rise of medical science, especially in Western countries. Infectious disease has disappeared as the main cause of death, to be replaced by the so-called diseases of senescence, especially diseases of the vascular system and cancer. At the same time, the average age of death both for men and women has been markedly increased. People are voluntarily controlling the size of their families, in spite of which a great many deaths occur at early ages as well as later in life from the new killer diseases. The Utopian state, when all will live to the natural age of death, is far from being achieved. The situation is particularly harrowing, since the early death of the breadwinner of a family, or the mother of young children, leaves them in a situation of difficulty and distress, and the deaths of young children are felt more keenly where families are smaller. The causes of these tragedies are being intensively studied, but undoubtedly the stress of modern life is one important underlying factor. Others may be unnatural food, an unnatural way of life, and lack of exercise in urban environments.

We shall in succeeding chapters proceed to a more detailed study of diseases of the vascular system and of cancer. Meanwhile, in the next chapter we shall look at the influence of the modern way of life on those diseases which are due to other basic causes, namely those of genetic and congenital origin.

8 GENETICS AND INHERITANCE

It is not our object in this work to recount the laws of inheritance, the general principles of which are well known. We do wish, however, to discover in what ways, if any, man's newer ways of life impart dangers to health or survival. It is often said that today we preserve the weak and unfit, and by so doing we are contributing to physical and mental decline; that in recent wars the flower of our nations' manhood has been destroyed, leaving the second-rate only to perpetuate the species; and that we are preserving sub-lethal genes, which will weaken the stock. On the face of it, there would appear to be some justification for these fears, but the problems are by no means simple. At the same time, rightly or wrongly, it is widely believed that a higher birth rate amongst ethnic groups of lesser mental endowment, and amongst those members of communities of lesser intelligence or mentally deficient, will lead to race deterioration. These problems too are of great complexity and the simpler and more straightforward interpretations may well be erroneous.

It cannot be denied that the world's inhabitants are divided into different ethnic groups with clear-cut and recognisable physical features by which they can be distinguished. It can also not be denied that advances in civilised ways of life are the result of the greater inventiveness and ingenuity of certain ethnic groups, who as a result tend to regard other members of the human race as backward. Whereas the situation with regard to the inheritance of physical features is simple, that with regard to mental ability is complex and the two must be considered separately.

The physical differences between ethnic groups are, on available evidence, of comparatively recent origin and are not based on any profound genetic differences. Australoid peoples, such as Australian aborigines, were at one time regarded as being of negroid type. It is, however, today realised that they possess characters which link them to the caucasoid and mongoloid peoples, and they are perhaps similar to a more primitive pattern from which other ethnic groups developed by 'genetic drift' in response to the conditions of their environment. They also possess features which more closely link them to man's closest ancestors, *Homo erectus*, as exemplified by the fossil Java man and Peking man. There is, however, no question that they belong to the family of *Homo sapiens* and share with other ethnic groups the same gene equipment and the same fundamental potentialities.

The closeness of the gene equipment amongst different ethnic groups is shown by what happens when intermarriage occurs between them. The most fertile field for investigation exists in the United States, where ethnic groups have intermingled over many generations, between caucasoids and negroids, caucasoids and mongoloids (Amerindians), and negroids and mongoloids. It is clear that the physical features of the different ethnic groups are inherited in a straightforward Mendelian fashion, and that no genes have become so strongly developed as to be predominant. This argues that the differences are of recent origin as stated above. To give a simple example: the caucasoid + negro cross produces mulatto children, who are intermediate in their ethnic characters between these two groups; if two mulattos mate, Mendel's first law—the law of segregation—operates, so that of 8 children, 2 are negro, 2 are caucasoid, and the rest are mulatto. Two negro children of such matings will produce negro children, and two caucasoids produce caucasoid children. The same rules apply with matings between all other ethnic groups, showing that, in spite of appearances, the physical differences between ethnic groups are genetically rather superficial. Such differences are accounted by 'genetic drift', which can be best explained by reference to an example from studies of African Green Monkeys, which were transferred to the island of St Kitts in the Caribbean only some 300 years ago.

Green Monkeys (*Cercopithecus aethiops sabaeus*) are widely distributed in West Africa and popular as pets. They were frequently taken across the Atlantic during the sugar boom in the West Indies and some reached St Kitts during the early seventeenth century. Some of these monkeys escaped and by 1680 free-ranging colonies had become established; indeed, they became so numerous that they became a pest, and were regarded as vermin with a bounty on their heads. They have, therefore, been established there for some 300 years, equivalent to some 75-100 monkey generations. During this time, certain definite morphological differences have been acquired by the St Kitts monkeys, which distinguish them from the parent African stock. These differences are seen in the skull and teeth and are therefore susceptible to measurement, and they have been described by Colyer (1936) and by Ashton and Zuckerman (1950, 1951a, 1951b). As with differences in the conformation of different ethnic groups of *Homo sapiens*, these changes are due to 'genetic drift', that is the action of selection on systems of multiple genes.

In human affairs, the maintenance of multiple systems of genes (a wide degree of genetic polymorphism) is of great importance, because multiple skills are required in our way of life. Different wildlife forms have developed different systems of mating. With grazing animals, such as horses or deer, the strongest male collects a herd of females and drives off other males. The progeny are thus sired by him alone, bear his imprint and carry his genes. An arrangement such as this leads to uniformity and is no doubt beneficial in the case of animals that are hunted. At the other extreme, wolves observe strict monogamy, so that the young wolves carry genes from different sires. Such an arrangement leads to diversity and greater adaptability. With chimpanzees, the females seem mostly to be common property when on heat, though the group leader sees to it that he is the first to mount the female: however, some tendency to a monogamous situation has at times been noted. Gibbons, on the other hand, which are also classified as Hominoidea, are strictly monogamous and live in family groups.

Evidence would suggest that primitive man adopted a rather loose monogamous system early in his history. His way of life demanded a diversity of skills which a rigid polygamy would deny. There is, however, no direct evidence of this, though Stone Age peoples who have survived to the present are mostly monogamous. Since the agricultural revolution, the system has been varied in a great many instances, probably as the result of the acquisition of personal property by certain individuals. The age of the patriarchs was accompanied by the acquisition of numerous wives and concubines, women being regarded as amongst the patriarchs' personal possessions. Indeed, the age of slavery had started also, and the lives of both men and women were regarded also amongst these possessions; young boys were castrated to provide eunuchs to guard the women and ensure that only the patriarch could reproduce his kind with them. It would be expected from this that the patriarchal line would stamp certain physical features on the progeny. Can one not perhaps discern both the physical features and the character of the early Hebrew patriarchs in the Jewish communities of today?

While, therefore, the main ethnic groups in man have come into being through genetic drift, some smaller groups with distinctive features may have come into being as a result of a change in the system of mating consequent on the acquisition of property. This tendency would be intensified because of the practice amongst propertied people of marrying near relatives as the principal wife to produce the hereditary line. However, other systems also arose, which have influenced human history, again associated with property inheritance. Importance was evidently attached to a continuance of inheritance through the blood line for the reason that the rulers were regarded as being descendants of the gods. One could be abundantly sure that the mother's children were of this blood, and so inheritance became matriarchal. From this arose the practice of brothers marrying their sisters, so as not to be deprived of what they regarded as their rights. This system prevailed in Egypt throughout her history until the fall of the last of the Ptolemys, Cleopatra. It undoubtedly accounted for some peculiarities of Egyptian history, the successive rise and fall of Egyptian power, and the continual rise of new dynasties, which again disappeared.

Interference throughout human history with random mating for the preservation of property or racial purity has had nothing but bad effects. Too much property has fallen into too few hands; class divisions have been intensified; and rulers have led their peoples into unnecessary wars for the sole purpose of increasing their own wealth and power. Where ethnic groups are mingled in a single country, tensions can only be increased by race segregation laws, which prevent their mixing in marriage if they so wish; such mixing will in time lead to more uniformity and more harmony.

In wild animal communities, natural laws of instinct promote exogamy, by which mating between closely related individuals is avoided. A stallion will drive out from his herd the colts and fillies of his own breeding and bring in others from outside. In primitive man, some similar system evidently prevailed, the relics of which are found in the totem system. To this day in Africa, a member of one totem clan, say the bushbuck, will owe loyalty and hospitality to another member of the same clan, but they will not intermarry. Members of the different clans are distributed intertribally and the system was evidently a means by which marriage with close blood relatives was avoided. In human history, since the nomadic life was abandoned and man settled in small agricultural and other communities, marriage between close relatives has been common. Amongst the upper classes, the reason was preservation of position and property, as we have seen. Amongst the poorer people, prior to the Industrial Revolution, communication between settlements and villages was so poor and travel so limited that there was a tendency for marriages to occur within the same village or group of villages. The result was a coupling of similar genes, some of which might be positively harmful; in any case the gene pool would be reduced. This problem has progressively disappeared since the Industrial Revolution, when travel has become so widespread.

We have seen that genetic drift can occur within a single wide system of genes. Also, however, gene mutations are continually occurring, the vast majority of them harmful. A gene is a unit of information, composed of a nucleic acid molecule made up of a thousand or so nucleotide pairs of deoxyribonucleic acid (DNA). Reproduction occurs when the two

DNA strands become unwound and separated from each other; each strand then replicates its missing complement. If each strand of DNA has 20 bases, the possible bits of information in each is 4^{20}, since there are four nitrogenous bases, adenine and guanine, which are purines, and cytosine and thymine, which are pyrimidines. Sequences of various patterns determine the genetic code. Mutations arise when there are mistakes in basic self-copying, for which there is obviously abundant scope. Each gene is responsible for the selection and assembly of the proper sequence of amino acids from the 20 available for the manufacture of essential proteins. When a mutation occurs, a structural error will follow. If present in a sex cell, this means that errors will occur in the development of the foetus. The genes are aligned on chromosomes, of which there are 46 in human body cells, but only half that number in the sex cells. The sex cells are produced by reduction division or meiosis in the following way. Initially, there are two rapid cell divisions, following which the paternal and maternal chromosomes become closely entwined with each other lengthwise, in such a way that the genes from each parent (alleles) are opposite each other. Each chromosome now doubles, so that there are four paired strands or 'chromatids'. The pairs now pull away somewhat from each other, so that the original two chromosomes separate. However, two of the four strands, one from each pair, have broken in one or more identical places, and the broken end of each strand has united with an end of the other strand. This is known as 'crossing over' and ensures that there has been an interchange of corresponding genes from the mother and father. In this way, offspring acquire mixed genes not only from the two parents, but also from the grandparents. It is this which accounts for the mixed features and characters of our young, which resemble neither parent, but are true mixed-up hybrids. Crossing-over may have occurred at hundreds of sites, so that no two spermatazoa or ova are ever precisely identical. Meiosis is completed by two successive divisions, so that haploid sex cells are produced. When two sex cells unite, an embryo is formed with diploid chromosome numbers. The genetic inheritance it receives determines the 'genotype', that is the genetic capability of the growing organism; this will be ordered and modified, as we shall see, by environmental factors, the interrelation of which with the genotype will determine the 'phenotype'.

The presence of mutated genes in one or both of the sex cells will produce varying results, depending on the nature of the gene. If the mutated gene is 'dominant', it will produce an abnormal character, in most cases undesirable. If the mutated gene is recessive, its effects will not be apparent in the heterozygous condition, but its possessor will be a 'carrier'. If two carriers produce children and a homozygous condition is produced by a junction of the two recessive mutated genes, then the offspring will not survive and the abnormal gene will disappear. In the case of recessive genes, there is an obviously greater risk of their becoming reduplicated when close relatives marry, and it is indeed the case that marriages between cousins produce an incidence of genetic defectives that is higher than normal. Conversely, marriages between persons from widely separated communities have a better chance of success in this respect. Indeed, it might be thought that recessive genes could become so diluted as to be unimportant. This occurs and is a strong argument against the claim that genetically unfit persons should be sterilised or otherwise prevented from breeding. Indeed, except in small communities, recessive mutant genes are unimportant and would in time disappear but for the continual re-appearance of mutant genes. It is, therefore, the re-appearance of these genes that constitutes the problem, and we have to consider whether the circumstances of civilised life are such as to augment the appearance of mutant genes. Regrettably, we shall find that this is so. Let us first briefly enumerate those genes, which have a lethal effect at any point between fertilisation and some point in later life. Amongst recessive lethal genes, some ten conditions are important, which include amaurotic idiocy, muscular dystrophies and other conditions which are incompatible with life. Some five conditions are described as semi-dominant lethals, which include spina bifida. Fully lethal genes mostly act on the embryo or foetus, causing its death or abortion.

Ashley Montagu, in his book *Human Heredity*, lists no less than 455 separate disorders of genetic origin. Some of the more important purely genetic diseases will be discussed later in this chapter. It is of obvious importance to recognise what conditions are due to purely genetic derangement, and what congenital abnormalities may be due to other causes and are therefore not heritable. It has further to be realised that genes merely provide a template for development and that their action may be profoundly modified by external factors. The final product, therefore—the 'phenotype'—is the result of interaction between heredity—the 'genotype'—and environment. The factors which influence the genotype are of two main orders: first, those experienced in the uterus before birth; second, those experienced after birth. Even within the uterus, the life of the foetus can be affected by external influences such as radiation or even loud sounds. Conversely, some fallacies resulting from defective genes, such as haemophilia, diabetes and pernicious anaemia can be corrected after birth by the supply of deficient chemicals; however, relief of such deficiencies will tend to increase the frequency of defective genes in the community. The action of genes in somatic cells is controlled by the surrounding cells, and the environment in the body can be modified by hormones, so that the same set of genes in different environments may result in a different expression of character. The genes can only do as much as their particular limits enable them to do within the limits of the material provided. The materials are provided by the environment, which influence the genetic material; the environments are: (1) intracellular, in which the genes interact with each other; (2) the intra-uterine; and (3) the extra-uterine. The same genotype in differing environments may give rise to quite different responses without the heritable properties of the genes being altered. Let us study these environments.

The Intra-Uterine Environment

The human embryo, that is up to eight weeks from conception, is extremely sensitive to changes not only in the mother, but in the external world also. The younger the embryo, the more likely is its development to be seriously affected by disturbing conditions which may cause structural and functional disorders or physical and mental defects. There are some ten factors which are of especial importance: (1) the age of the mother; (2) previous child-bearing experience of the mother; (3) any disability of the mother; (4) antigenic sensitivities of the mother; (5) nutritional effects; (6) infections; (7) drugs; (8) physical agents; (9) emotional factors; and (10) other environmental factors. Many such disturbing influences are plainly liable to arise as a result of urban living, and it is necessary to examine these factors individually in this light.

Maternal Age

The human female can normally conceive some 3 years after the commencement of menstruation, that is at about 16½ years of age. Miscarriages and stillbirths are very common in very young mothers, who also suffer the highest mortality rates in childbirth and bear more deformed children. The most favourable period for childbirth is from age 21 to 28. From 29 onwards, maternal and infant mortality rates tend to rise; stillbirths and miscarriages increase, and there is a rise in the numbers of defective children born. This trend is increased after the age of 35, when there is a sudden increase in the number of defective children born, especially mongols and hydrocephalic babies.

Previous Child-Bearing Experience

The birth weight and size of babies increase with the number of previous pregnancies. The first-born and latest-born foetuses are those least likely to survive, and foetal malformations are more common. It is clear, then, that the number of previous pregnancies has an influence on the development of the embryo, and modern tendencies to limitation and delay in parturition could contribute both to poor breeding performance and the proportion of deformed babies born.

Maternal Disabilities

Any non-infectious disabilities from which the mother may suffer are likely to affect the development of the foetus. Hypertension, for example, causes a high rate of foetal loss and maternal mortality. Diabetes, including prediabetes, also affects the foetus. Children of prediabetic mothers usually weigh over 9 lb. at birth, and children of prediabetic fathers also tend to be overweight. When the mother is clinically diabetic, the foetus grows very rapidly, attaining the birth weight long before term so that there is a high incidence of dystokia; indeed, in such conditions still-births and new-born deaths may reach 50 per cent; such incidents may precede by many years the development of clinical diabetes. Hyper-thyroidism also adversely affects the foetus and may be the cause of 30 per cent foetal deaths; conversely, hypothyroidism can cause goitre and cretinism in the infant. Toxaemias or haemorrhage may affect brain development, so that the children are mentally retarded or present behaviour problems in later life.

Antigenic Sensitivities

Where the genes of mother and foetus differ, the surface antigens of the foetal red blood cells may sensitise the mother against the baby's red cells. The result, where this happens, is anaemia of the foetus, which develops at a late foetal age. This results from the presence in the foetal blood of the so-called rhesus factor, but its absence from the mother. There are at least ten major genes involved, possibly more. The first child of an Rh− woman by an Rh+ man suffers no ill-effects, but the mother may have become sensitised during the pregnancy, so that subsequent children are at risk. Sometimes stillbirths result, but if born alive the infant suffers from anaemia or jaundice (*erythroblastosis foetalis*), from which it dies in hours or days, unless an exchange transfusion of the entire baby's blood is performed. This, of course, only occurs in infants who have acquired an Rh+ factor from the father. Fortunately, all mothers do not become sensitised; if they did, a great many more babies (1/17 or 1/18) would suffer, whereas the actual incidence is only 1/200. Very occasionally, similar accidents occur also in connection with the ABO blood-group system. Babies sometimes also become sensitised to other proteins, such as egg albumin, consumed by the mother to excess.

Nutritional Effects

The nutrition of the foetus is dependent on that of the mother; the foetus is also affected by her occupation, health, general hygiene and the sanitary conditions in which she lives. Factors such as these generally reflect the social and economic status of the family. Higher infant mortality rates are experienced in families where living conditions are poor, and basic organic deficiencies can affect a child's later development. In the early stages of foetal growth, defective maternal nutrition can be decisive in producing certain physical abnormalities, usually because of the lack of some vitamins, fatty acids or proteins. Malformed foetuses are common where vitamins B, C and D are deficient; foetal rickets, for example, is common amongst the peasantry in poorer countries, especially where the women are in purdah and denied access to sunlight. Such deficiencies in the mother are usually sub-clinical, so that it is difficult to correlate cause and effect. Cow's milk is deficient in the longer-chain unsaturated fatty acids, essential for the development of the large human brain, unless it is fortified correctly. In all milk substitutes there are dangers of such deficiencies and they are a poor substitute for breast-feeding. It is plain from this that a child's mental potential may already be impaired during foetal life, and this is an important factor in the perennial nature-versus-nurture element in the controversial IQ studies.

Infections

Some pathogenic organisms, including viruses, bacteria and protozoa, can pass the placenta to the foetus. During the first three months of pregnancy viral infections can seriously affect the orderly progress of development; bacteria and protozoa do not give rise to developmental abnormalities but can seriously affect the foetus, causing its death or abortion. Foetuses can, however, be protected passively against viral infections by means of vaccines and the immunity will last for several months after birth. Infections which especially affect the foetus are poliomyelitis, smallpox—as was known to Edward Jenner—chicken pox, measles, mumps, scarlet fever, erysipelas, and recurrent (relapsing) fever. It is believed also that the myxovirus of Influenza A can produce serious

deformities in the embryo. German measles ('rubella'), acquired during
the first twelve weeks of pregnancy, causes gross developmental defects
or—in 12-20 per cent of cases—foetal death; the survivors suffer also
from cataract, deafness and mental defects.

Syphilis, if passed to the foetus early in pregnancy, causes miscarriage;
if acquired later in pregnancy, the child suffers from congenital syphilis,
blindness, deafness, or defects of the heart; sometimes, however, the
disease only manifests itself later in life in severe disorders of the nervous
system. With tuberculosis, the foetal death rate is also high, and infants
born of tubercular mothers usually die within twelve months of birth.

Amongst protozoal diseases, infants can be born with malaria. Congenital cases of toxoplasmosis suffer from severe disorders of the nervous system and eyes, in particular meningo-encephalo-myelitis, micro-
phthalmia, chorioretinitis, microcephaly, hydrocephalus, convulsions,
idiocy and mental retardation. Some congenital cancers also occur, such
as malignant melanoma and chorio-carcinoma.

Congenital malformations are the second-highest cause of deaths in
unborn babies. About 23 per cent of the human race dies before birth
or shortly after.

Drugs

As might be expected, drugs taken by the mother affect the foetal
environment. Amongst the many ill-effects attributed to the use of tobacco, it is said that heavy smoking habits by the mother will or can lead
to premature birth of the baby. Barbiturates used at childbirth can kill
the child from asphyxia. The use of drugs in pregnancy, even those commonly taken at other times, may have effects varying from those that
are virtually inapparent to gross defects of development. Expectant
mothers suffering from the discomforts of early pregnancy often request
their doctors to supply them with some form of relief and many doctors
will oblige if they can, perhaps sometimes against their better judgement.
This was the situation which led to the Thalidomide tragedies. Thalidomide was outstanding in the relief it gave to the discomforts of pregnancy; unfortunately, during a critical period between the 27th and
40th days from conception it has a profound effect on foetal development; it can even cause damage up to 90 days. It was some time before
the relationship between the use of Thalidomide and the birth of grossly
deformed babies came to be realised, and during that time hundreds of
crippled children were born destined to survive but lacking one or more
of their limbs. Thalidomide had been exhaustively tested for safety
before being placed on the market. Previously, drugs were not routinely

tested on pregnant animals before release for general use by the medical profession. This situation has now been corrected; however, knowledge of the effects of drugs in general use on the developing foetus is still deficient. To what extent the use of drugs during pregnancy may be responsible for backward and difficult children cannot be said, but it could be one factor responsible for the high proportion of unteachable children and illiterates in the schools.

Physical Agents

Malformations of the foetus may be caused by a number of unfortunate circumstances, which could be described as accidents. Such are any pressure changes in the uterus, whether caused by internal or external forces. Deformity may result from faulty position of the foetus, its immobilisation, mechanical shaking and temperature changes. Massive doses of X-rays during the first two months of pregnancy may cause abortion; alternatively they may cause a number of developmental defects, such as microcephalic idiocy, hydrocephalus, defects of the nervous system, premature birth, mental deficiency and stillbirth. Apart from such gross and unfortunate effects, the foetus is affected to a surprising degree by physical factors in the external environment. A foetus will respond in a convulsive and startled way to sudden loud noises or vibrations; sound reaching it in any form elicits increased activity.

Finally, of course, the infant is subject to birth injuries.

Emotional Factors

Emotional disturbances in the mother may influence both the structural and psychological development of the foetus. One may perhaps include in the emotional sphere the demand on doctors for tranquillising agents during pregnancy such as led to the Thalidomide tragedies. In this sense, mothers themselves must be held partly to blame. The pressures of modern society are such that many suffer from varying degrees of stress, which have undesirable effects on the unborn children. Cleft palate is one defect which has been associated with emotional disturbances of the mother during the first ten weeks of pregnancy. During stress, some cortical hormones can cross the placenta into the foetal circulation, and excess hydro-cortisone activity is believed to be the cause of cleft palate. Emotional factors during pregnancy can also be the cause of psychological and psychosomatic irritability occurring after birth, which persist to older ages. Emotional factors are also an important cause of habitual miscarriages and sterility.

Other Environmental Factors

In a modern world, expectant mothers are subjected to so many environmental influences that one cannot wonder at the high proportion of foetuses which fail to survive or are in some way affected physically or mentally in after life. Of greatest importance is to discern in all cases whether the defect is fundamental, due to gene deficiency. Is the template defective, or has the developmental craftsman failed in his construction of the model? With known genetic disorders, this is easily determined, but with many conditions such as low intelligence or mental subnormality, the answer is so elusive as to be virtually impossible to determine. However, the craftsman's work is not ended with the birth of the child, since the environment after birth is of equal importance. This we must now study.

The Environment After Birth

Mothering

Even when a baby is born genetically and physically sound, it may fail to grow and develop normally if its mothering is inadequate; it may even die during the first or second year of life. Neglected babies are pale and wrinkled and the eyes are dull and lack lustre. Either they lie quiet and motionless, or they cry for hours on end, regurgitate their food, suffer from diarrhoea, cease to grow, and suffer from mental deterioration. Amongst those that survive, emotionally starved children fail in learning to speak, walk or feed themselves. Indeed, any child that has been starved of love during the first six years of life is likely to be severely handicapped for the rest of its existence. In a child's personalisation process there are three critical developmental periods: (1) *0-6 months*, when a co-operative relationship is developed with a specific person, normally the mother; (2) *to the end of the third year*, when the child needs the ever-present support and companionship of the mother or mother-figure; (3) *4th to 5th years*, when the child learns to maintain a relationship with the mother or mother-figure for a few days or even weeks of absence. Inadequacies of mothering during these vital periods can have lasting physical and psychological effects, even bone growth being affected. These defects may be described as psychosomatic, the child sensing that normal love and affection are lacking.

The 'battered baby syndrome' would appear to be a phenomenon apart from the neglectful and resentful mother. Battered babies are not necessarily neglected babies. Mothers who assault their babies often do so under the influence of a compulsive urge over which they have no control, and are subsequently bitterly ashamed of themselves. Animals, as all zoo keepers know, either the sire or the dam, often assault and kill their young. The urge to do so may well be deep-rooted in nature and arise from some inborn instinct to be rid of young which cannot be supported.

Physical Development

The rate of growth in children is affected by the economic conditions of the parents, being slowest in families living in poor circumstances. Sickness and mortality rates also are higher in homes where conditions of life are poor; this disparity appears during the first week of life and increases to become 3-4 times greater in the poorest families. These differences are not genetic, but due to poorer conditions of nutrition and sanitation. They are of greater importance than might be supposed and have been studied extensively amongst immigrant families in the United States. It was at one time supposed that Slavic immigrants were inferior to Anglo-Saxon, both physically and mentally; however, the undoubted initial differences disappeared in one or two generations, extending even to changes of skeletal and skull conformation.

Environment and Mental Ability

One of ten persons in many Western countries, including the United States, is mentally ill. One of the burning questions of the day asks how far mental ability is linked to genes and how far to environment? The question is unresolved and subject to bitter debate. That genius exists in some people cannot be rationally disputed, nor that bright parents on the whole produce bright children. Would Mozart ever have displayed his precocious musical talents, had he not been reared against a musical background? Nevertheless, his production of major musical works before he entered his teens argues that he was genetically endowed with exceptional musical talents, though they might never have been displayed if a suitable environment had been lacking. There is, however, no reliable test for intelligence, because it is impossible to define intelligence. No group of Western peoples could survive in the environment of the Australian aborigines; however, the aborigines can and do survive in pampered Western environments. Maybe Western children could survive if reared with aboriginal families, and it could be argued that, as a result of a higher mental endowment, they could better life for the aborigines by introducing advanced techniques. American Indian children score equally with white children in IQ tests once their backgrounds have been equalised. The American Indians are—or were—a Stone Age people and we have to conclude that Stone Age peoples, or some Stone Age peoples, possessed a mental genetical inheritance equal to those of the Western world. Indeed, it is incomprehensible that the genes permitting technical advance into the space age were not already present in the ancestors of the Western peoples who achieved it. However, the IQ test is loaded to ascertain 'fitness' for a certain environment, no more. Performance in IQ tests is lower in lower social groups, but improves when children from these groups are brought up with families of higher economic status. These tests are invariably slanted to a certain cultural background and test 'fitness' for that environment.

Twins, Genes and Environment

The best chance of assessing accurately the relative influence of genetic constitution and environment on performance rests with the study of identical twins who have been separated in early life. Such studies have been made, notably in the United States, where—it is to be noted—multiple births are more frequent in negroes at 14 per thousand as against 10 per thousand in whites. In that country, 40,000 pairs of twins are born each year, of which 13,000 are identical or monozygotic. The frequency of monozygotic twins is the same for negroes and whites, and indeed throughout the world. Results of such studies in relation to the studies of intelligence are disappointing, perhaps partly because identical twins rarely show great intellectual achievement. Moreover, twins, when parted, usually go to families of similar cultural background. When reared in different cultural backgrounds, similar physical characteristics are retained, though height, size and shape may vary somewhat; they do, however, vary greatly in poise and outlook. When reared by families of similar background, they resemble each other greatly in morphology, ability and psychological traits. Homosexuality is usually present in both identical twins, but is thought to arise in the main from environmental causes. Certain mental disorders of known genetic origin more frequently affect both identical twins than non-identical. Such are schizophrenia, manic-depressive psychosis, and involutional psychosis. In the two former, the concordance in identical twins is 90 per cent, whereas the incidence of schizophrenia and manic-depressive psychosis in the general population is only one in two hundred; this shows clearly the influence of a dominant gene. With involutional psychosis the concordance in identical twins is 61 per cent, whereas the frequency in the general population is 3-7 per thousand; the etiology of this condition is unlikely to rest with a single gene; though of genetic origin, environmental factors may also be involved and the causes are obscure. In epilepsy, the concordance in identical twins is more than 66 per cent as against only 3 per cent in non-fraternal; this would suggest that epilepsy is usually the result of genetic causes.

This leaves us with little evidence relating to the inheritance of intelligence and ability. If one identical twin shows criminal tendencies, there is a 70 per cent chance that the other is also a criminal. With non-identical twins, the chance is 30 per cent. However, the difference is not so striking as might appear. Identical twins are always of the same sex, whereas non-identical twins are not, and their life-styles, intimacy and sharing of habits are greater. It is usually believed that criminality arises from social conditions and is not of genetic origin.

Genes and Constitution

It should be clear from what has been written that an individual's constitution depends on the effect of environmental circumstances on a fundamental genetic pattern. Civilisation, urbanisation, crowding and unnatural living conditions have the effect of magnifying the environmental influences to the extent that the basic genetic pattern becomes masked and is not easily discernible. Studies on identical twins have on the whole been unrewarding, but it would appear to this writer that comparative studies of the careers of non-identical twins of the same sex reared in identical circumstances would be of value in showing to what extent inherited abilities may vary. For example, in the animal kingdom a litter of 5 or 6 wolves will produce individuals of varying temperaments and abilities; some will be aggressive and dominate their sibs; others will be affectionate but retiring. The future pack leaders have been genetically selected before birth in a situation in which environmental factors can be largely discounted.

In man, it is virtually impossible to disentangle the effects of genes and environment either as ethnic groups or as between individuals, and in this work we shall certainly not attempt to do so. Some individuals, nevertheless, are placed at a disadvantage because of inherited genetic defects, which require to be distinguished from non-inheritable congenital defects acquired during uterine life. Diabetes, for example, is associated with defects in a pair of recessive genes, and one in four diabetics come from the same family as other diabetics; it can also arise *de novo* from adverse emotional states and over-eating. With tuberculosis, there is a hereditary diathesis—that is an inherited susceptibility. Phenylketonuria is an inherited recessive disorder of metabolism, in which the liver fails to convert phenylalanine to tyrosine. Damage to the nervous system occurs during the first six months of life, resulting in intellectual impairment. The incidence of this condition is 1/25,000 persons; in the heterozygous condition sufferers appear to be normal, though their conversion of phenylalanine is impaired; the homozygotes are clinically affected, and require to be fed on diets low in alanine. Numerous other examples could be cited, including hypertension, pernicious anaemia and some cancers which are believed to be genetically linked. However, let us study those conditions and diseases associated with sex differences.

From the time of conception, through uterine and new-born life and all through life, male mortality is higher than female. At conception, 120-150 fertilised eggs acquire the male Y chromosome as against 100 acquiring the female X chromosome; yet only 105 males are born to every 100 females, indicating that the intra-uterine death rate of males is 50 per cent higher than that of females. The best-known sex-linked disease is that of haemophilia, best known because of transmission through Queen Victoria of Britain to most of the royal families of Europe with terrible and far-reaching consequences. Females, possessing two X chromosomes, do not suffer from the disease, but their male progeny inheriting an affected X chromosome together with a paternal Y are clinical sufferers. The gene, which promotes colour blindness, is also situated on the X chromosome; females carrying two affected X chromosomes are all colour-blind, but not if they carry one affected chromosome; all males with an affected X are colour-blind, since the Y does not override it. There are ten to twenty other serious conditions attributed to incompletely sex-linked genes. Some other conditions are sex-influenced; in these the controlling genes are located in the autosomes—the non-sex chromosomes, but their dominance is controlled by genes on the sex chromosomes.

Another group of inherited traits is described as sex-linked. Such traits are expressed in one sex but not in another. They may be carried either on the autosomes or on the sex chromosomes, and they are hormone-dependent; they can affect both sexes but to a different degree. For example, males grow facial hairs, as beards or moustaches; females normally do not, though the hairs are present but do not develop. In males, baldness appears in varying degree in more than 40 per cent of persons over 34 years of age. A male carrying two baldness genes transmits baldness to all the sons; if he carries only one baldness gene, he transmits it to only half his sons. However, baldness can appear in male offspring, when neither parent shows signs of baldness if each parent contributes one baldness gene. Baldness may also be due to stress or disease arising from hormonal factors acting on gene function. Baldness is, of course, a distressing condition, particularly in young males. It is present in other primates, both apes and monkeys, especially chimpanzees, where it is seen in both sexes. Its onset cannot be prevented, since it is of purely genetic origin. The inheritance is simple, as shown in Table 8.1.

Table 8.1

Genotype	Males	Females
BB	Bald	Thinning or partial baldness
Bb	Bald	Non-bald
bb	Non-bald	Non-bald

B = dominant baldness gene
b = non-bald gene

Another sex-limited genetic condition is gout. The gout gene is dominant and carried on the autosomes, but gout only develops in 5 per cent of females as against 95 per cent of males. Some recessive disorders more frequently expressed in males than females are albinism, alkaptonuria, retinitis pigmentosa and amaurotic idiocy. Recessives more frequently expressed in females are diabetes, manic-depressive psychosis, Sydenham's chorea and Niemann-Pick disease. Many recessive genes are classified amongst the 'lethal genes', but are only lethal, of course, in the homozygous state, where the individual has received one such gene from each parent. Table 8.2 gives a list of the more important recessive and semi-dominant 'lethal gene' diseases.

Table 8.2

RECESSIVE LETHALS

(1) Niemann-Pick disease—an acute ichiopathic anthomatosis (yellowing of skin and tissues). There is a great enlargement of the spleen and liver accompanying the discolouration of the skin.
(2) Amaurotic idiocy (a) infantile (b) juvenile—impairment of vision leading to total blindness, degeneration of the nervous system, idiocy.
(3) Degeneration of cerebral white matter—(a) acute infantile (b) sub-acute juvenile (c) convulsive.
(4) Epidermolysis bullosa—blisters forming on the skin with light pressure.
(5) Gargoylism—multiple growth derangement, gargoyle face.
(6) Glioma retinae—tumour of the retina.
(7) Ichthyosis foetalis—scaling of the skin.
(8) Infantile muscular dystrophy—muscle-wasting with paralysis.
(9) Microphthalomia of the sex-linked type—small eyes.
(10) Pseudo-hypertrophic muscular dystrophy—muscular enlargement and paralysis.

SEMI-DOMINANT LETHALS
(11)   Minor Bradydactyly—short fingers.
(12)   Pelger's nuclear anomaly—unsegmented leucocytes.
(13)   Sebaceous cysts—cystic tumours of sebaceous glands.
(14)   Spina bifida—congenital cleft of the vertebral column.
(15)   Telangiectasis—dilation of capillaries; serious nose-bleeding.

Finally, brief notice must be taken of a group of conditions and diseases associated with the chromosomal anomalies, which mostly occur during meiosis and 'crossing over'. These arise from the possession of absent or excess sex chromosomes or fragmentation or injury to autosomes. The normal sex of any person and aberrations of the sex chromosomes are easily determined, in most cases because of the behaviour of the sex chromosomes. In the female, only one X chromosome is fully functional and acts as an autosome; the other paired X in all body cells curls up on itself and is deposited as a chromatin body on the inside of the nuclear membrane, known as the Barr body. This is easily seen under the microscope and so the sex of the person from whom the cells are derived can be determined and it can also be determined if excess X chromosomes are present. Barr bodies are present in foetal cells from the 18th day of development, so that aspiration of cells in amniotic fluid (amniocentesis) can reveal the sex of the foetus.

After birth, anomalies of sex chromosomes can also be determined in this way, as is shown in Table 8.3. Accidents in meiosis or conjugation

Table 8.3

NORMAL		CHROMOSOMAL ABERRATIONS				
Male XY	Female XX	XO	Xx	XX XXY	XXX XXXY	XXXX

of the gametes are not uncommon and are of greater or lesser importance. Some of the commoner disabilities are listed below.

Klinefelter's Syndrome

Sufferers from this condition have the chromosomal constitution XXY: they possess an extra X chromosome, though the possession of the Y makes them male. As seen from the table, the extra X chromosome is not deposited and so is functional. Though males, such persons have small sterile testes and feminine characters; there is feminine develop- ment of the breasts (gynaecomastia). There is also mental retardation.

Turner's Syndrome

In this condition, the patient has inherited only one sex chromosome, the female X giving the constitution XO. The ovaries fail to develop and no ova are ever produced. There are also physical and sometimes psycho- logical abnormalities.

Superfemale

Persons so affected possess three X chromosomes, XXX. The breasts are underdeveloped and the external genitalia remain infantile. The vagina is small and the menopause comes early.

Down's Syndrome (Mongolism)

One of the most distressing of all the chromosomal abnormalities is that of the mongol child. The condition is due to a fracture during develop- ment (meiosis) of chromosome 22, which breaks into two. Mongol children rarely survive to breeding age, so that in the vast majority of cases the condition arises from an accident in the maturation of the gamete and is not heritable. These accidents occur more commonly when the mother is older, especially if she has not previously borne children. Mongols have 47 chromosomes in place of the usual 46. Very occasionally, cases occur when Down's Syndrome is combined with Klinefelter, when there are 48 chromosomes, an extra female X to- gether with an extra autosome. In Turner's syndrome, there are only 45 chromosomes, since one of the X chromosomes or the Y is missing. However, in this condition the number of chromosomes in the body cells is variable, so as to give—in genetic terms—a 'mosaic' condition. One cell line is always XO, but others may be XX, XY, XYY or XXX. This shows that the error occurred early in cell division and not during maturation of the gametes, that is during the vulnerable first 28 days. Nevertheless, affected individuals are always feminine in type and of short stature. This shows that the Y chromosome, though sometimes believed to be relatively inert, performs a function in determining male characters.

Sex Reversal

This is most commonly due to the 'testicular feminisation syndrome'. In this, apparent females are in reality sex-reversed males; the sex is XY and the cells are chromatin-negative. The condition is hereditary and transmitted through the female line either as a sex-linked recessive or dominant. The individual is apparently female in the appearance of the external genitalia and of the body; the axillary and pubic hair is scanty. However, there is no menstruation and the vagina is incompletely developed. The testes remain in the abdomen, the inguinal canal or the labia majora. The epididymis and vas deferens are present on both sides, but there may also be a rudimentary uterus and fallopian tubes.

Abnormal metabolism of the maternal or placental hormones before the gonads of the embryo are differentiated may also lead to sex reversal. Excessive secretion of progesterone or testosterone may masculinise a female embryo, leading to its development as a male, a hermaphrodite, or an intersexual pseudo-hermorphrodite. A survey in Canada showed that some 1/400 phenotype males may in fact be genotype females. Male to female sex reversal may occur in the same way but the incidence is lower; some 1/2,000 females may be genotype males.

Radiation and Mutation

We have found that an individual's phenotype, both physical and psychological depend: (1) on the inherited genotype and (2) on the environment before and after birth. In wild animals—and in man before urbanisation—environmental factors were relatively unimportant, but since urbanisation have become increasingly more important to such an extent that it is difficult to ascertain the fundamental influences of the genotype. Plainly, the environment is greatly variable, and, the more complex becomes civilised life, the more variable it becomes. We have seen also that the chromosomal pattern, the karyotype, is also variable because of accidents in maturation of the gametes or because of errors of cell division in the embryo; hormonal dysfunction in the mother can also lead to sexual abnormalities in the offspring. There are also influences which act directly on the genes, causing mutations. Most mutations have adverse effects, but some few at very rare intervals introduce favourable, heritable, factors into the stock, and are believed to be the fundamental mechanism of evolution. Such mutations have been occurring since genes and chromosomes were evolved, but our enquiry demands that we consider any evidence that mutations have become more frequent under modern conditions of living and, if so, whether the effects are harmful or beneficial. We also need to consider the factors which induce these mutations to occur. There is no evidence for the emergence of a new race of supermen either in the physical or intellectual sense, and so we can conclude that any mutations which have or are occurring in the human race are harmful rather than beneficial.

Studies are showing that the DNA of human cells is not pure and unadulterated human DNA. Some viruses can penetrate the DNA and replace human genes with viral genes. Such viruses are almost universally present in the human and animal genetic material, where they are normally quite harmless. Nevertheless, under certain conditions they could be responsible for abnormal behaviour of the cells leading, on the one hand, to conditions such as cancer and, on the other, to gene mutations and to the acquisition of new characters. There is no evidence that such occurs, but the possibility is being suggested by responsible scientists. We are, however, on more solid ground when we study the influence of radiation on genetic material, since it is well known, from studies on fruit flies, *Drosophila*, and other creatures, that mutations of genes occur at a predictable rate and that one major influence which causes it is radiation.

Radiation is a natural hazard to which all living things have been exposed since life began. Natural sources are radium or uranium, which disintegrate naturally, but of far greater importance are the well-known cosmic rays from outer space to which we are all exposed. The effects of radiation are greatest in the sex cells, in which it promotes mutations which can be heritable. There are various types of radiation, some of which are more harmful than others. Beta rays are free electrons, carrying a negative electric charge; alpha particles are the nuclei of helium atoms and carry two protons and two neutrons; gamma rays, the most deadly, are electromagnetic radiations of very high energy with great penetrating power; X-rays are similar to gamma rays and are produced by high-energy electrons. These radiations, in varying degree, are ionising; they collide with atoms, causing them to disintegrate, leaving electrically charged atoms or molecules, electrons being gained or lost so that they are unstable; this is ionisation. Ionisation leads to death of cells or genetic change. Radiation is measured in roentgens (r). One r corresponds to 2 ionisations per cubic micron, which equals 10^{17} ionisations for the whole body. Natural radiation received on average in one year is 0.1 r, of which a quarter comes from cosmic rays, one half from soil and rocks, and the balance from radioactive elements in the body, chiefly potassium. Unnatural sources of radiation are illuminated discs on watches, clocks and car dashboards, medical and dental X-rays, fluoroscopes and other artificial sources. Fall-out from weapons tests, nuclear power stations and so on is relatively insignificant, but radiation from luminous car clocks—absurd as it may seem—has with some formulations of luminous materials been so high as to reach danger levels, having regard to the proximity of these instruments to the genital organs of the driver and his passenger.

There are approximately 75 dominant mutations which occur spontaneously in man; most are detrimental and 80 per cent are lethal to the foetus, so that two in ten survive to be passed to succeeding generations; of these some cause sterility and so are unimportant in a genetic sense.

These mutations usually only operate in the homozygous state, so the incidence depends on the chance mating of two persons who suffer from the same mutation. Genetic damage is proportional to the mutation rate, which is proportional to the radiation dosage received. Thus, an increase of 5 per cent in the radiation rate results in 5 per cent more mutations. Older parents have been exposed to radiation over a longer period and have thus suffered from more mutations, since the effect is cumulative. The total accumulated dose of radiation received in 30 years of life has been calculated, and is given in Table 8.4. High scrotal temperatures

Table 8.4

Background radiation (cosmic rays etc.)	4.35
Medical X-rays	3.05
Fall-out (weapons tests etc.)	0.15
(luminous paints etc. ignored)	
Total	7.55

from wearing trousers also cause a significant number of mutations. Radiation can also cause burns, cancer and leukaemia.

In the United States and other Western countries, some 4-5 per cent of all children born alive suffer from defects such as mental deficiency, epilepsy, congenital malformations, neuro-muscular disorders, disorders of the blood, glandular systems, skin, skeleton, gastro-intestinal or genito-urinary systems. Of these, some 2 per cent—that is in the USA some 2 millions of total live births—are genetic and appear before sexual maturity. This figure is double that which would be expected in a primitive community—doubling the radiation rate would double the number of genetic defectives.

What then is the effect of civilisation on man in relation to genetic and congenital disabilities? Scientists disagree, but surely the facts speak for themselves? In spite of the confusion, there can be no doubt about certain facts: (1) the civilised way of life leads to an increase in

the numbers of babies born with physical and mental handicap; (2) it
contributes to the survival of handicapped persons; (3) the survival of
some genes, which are deleterious, especially those which are sex-linked
or recessive can be prolonged and they can cause trouble in later generations and indeed—as in the case of haemophilia—have had profound
historical consequences; (4) it is important to distinguish between disabilities of genetic and congenital origin.

It would appear obviously desirable that persons carrying deleterious
genes should not reproduce. Nevertheless, such genes, especially if recessive, will disappear of themselves, provided that marriage of close relatives
is avoided. They would in time disappear completely, were it not that
they regularly re-appear as a result of new mutations, and as we have
seen that modern ways of life have accelerated the rate at which these
mutations appear. One price that must be paid for a comfortable and
civilised way of life, together with a greatly increased average longevity,
is at present that there will always be too many persons who are dis-
advantaged from genetic or congenital causes. Ashley-Montagu, discus-
sing the case for and against Eugenics, lists the following as candidates
for sterilisation:

Insane: Lucretius, Isaac Newton, Nathaniel Lee, Strindberg, van Gogh,
  Nietzsche, Pushkin, Emily Dickinson.
Criminal tendencies: Villon, Verlaine, Rimbaud, Oscar Wilde, O'Henry,
  Baudelaire.
Epileptic: Dostoievsky, Conrad, van Gogh, Julius Caesar.
Inebriate or addicted to drugs: Tennyson, Coleridge, Lamb, de Quincy,
  Poe, Modigliani, Dylan Thomas.
Diseased: Gibbon, Rousseau, Keats, Pope, Pasteur, D.H. Lawrence,
  Robert Louis Stevenson, Elizabeth Barrett Browning, F.D. Roose-
  velt, Marcel Proust.
Blind: Homer, Milton, Helen Keller, Louis Braille.
Deaf: Beethoven, Helen Keller, Edison.
Deformed: Pope, Robert Hooke, Byron, Charles Steinettz, Toulouse-
  Lautrec.
Ne'er-do-weels: Socrates, Diogenes, Shelley, St Augustine, Gauguin,
  Thoreau.
Homeless: Jesus, van Gogh.
Tramps: Vachel Lindsay, W.H. Davies, Walt Whitman, George Orwell.
Paupers: Jesus, Gandhi, van Gogh, Francis Thompson.

9 CARDIO-VASCULAR DISEASE—HORROR AND DISMAY

Cancer and diseases of the cardio-vascular system, notably coronary thrombosis and stroke, are classed as diseases of senescence with doubtful justification, as we have seen earlier. Coronary troubles can affect young people, even in their twenties, and some cancers, notably the leukaemias, can affect very young persons from around 8 years old. Both groups of diseases can affect persons of all ages, and it seems more rational to regard them as responses of man to the unnatural environment he has adopted, as with the other diseases already discussed. Both groups of diseases have come into especial prominence during the past thirty years, because they now head the league of death causes in Westernised societies, cardio-vascular disease beating cancer by a short head. They achieved this doubtful distinction when mastery over infectious diseases was attained with the introduction of sulpha drugs and anti-biotics, and particularly when pneumonia and tuberculosis were overcome.

With the eclipse of the infectious diseases, the dangerous potential of the so-called diseases of senescence came to be better realised. Formerly, of course, young children had been dying in their teens of leukaemia, but a great many more had died of tuberculosis, diphtheria, poliomyelitis and other infectious conditions, so that the leukaemia problem seemed a minor one in comparison. Fathers of young families had been dying in their fifties of coronary heart disease, and mothers of stroke; but here again so many more died of pneumonia, tuberculosis and puerperal infections, that the diseases of senescence seemed unimportant in comparison. Once these diseases adopted their present role, the medical profession was nonplussed. To their members, it seemed unreasonable that, having resolved their major problems, a new family of diseases should appear to thwart their efforts. In the sphere of both cancer and cardio-vascular disease, there has been little apparent progress during the past thirty years. I have been closely associated during the past twenty years with researches into both groups of diseases, and what follows will reflect to some extent my personal experience during this time, first as pathologist to the London Zoo, and subsequently as Head of the Pathology Department at the Nuffield Institute of Comparative Medicine, the Zoological Society's research foundation, which is also at the London

Zoo. In this chapter, we consider cardio-vascular disease; cancer follows in the next.

There are, of course, many diseases which affect various parts of the cardio-vascular system. Hypertensive conditions have been mentioned in relation to stress; there is also a more serious form of hypertension, known as 'essential hypertension', in which the kidneys fail in their endocrine function of regulating blood pressure levels. In this survey, I shall confine myself to two interrelated disorders, which are responsible for coronary heart disease and stroke. These are arteriosclerosis, in particular that form known as 'atherosclerosis', and intravascular clotting, the blockage of arteries by blood clots. Another term used is 'arteriolo-sclerosis', that is sclerosis of very small arteries or arterioles, which are commonly affected in the kidneys and may be one cause of 'essential hypertension'.

The term 'sclerosis' means hardening and reflects the popular term 'hardening of the arteries'. Atheroma is derived from the Greek word for porridge, and describes the appearance and consistency of deposits in the artery walls. The atheromatous lesions or 'plaques' affect the narrow inner coats of arteries, which have three coats in the wall. The outer coat is known as the 'tunica adventitia', inside which is the 'tunica media'. The inner coat is the 'tunica intima'. This coat consists of a single layer of 'endothelium' or lining cells, beneath which are scanty cellular elements including some smooth muscle cells; it is separated from the 'tunica media' by a tough layer of elastic fibres, known as the 'internal elastic lamina'. The 'tunica media' is a much thicker coat composed largely of elastic fibres or smooth muscle, depending on the artery. The outer coat consists of loose connective tissue, which conveys the chief blood vessels and nerves of the artery.

The first sign of atheroma in an artery appears in a condition known as 'fatty streaking', caused by a diffuse deposit of lipid (fatty material) in the artery's inner coat. This is easily demonstrated in an artery from a dead animal by dipping it in a stain that colours fat; that known as Sudan IV is usually employed, and it imparts a red stain to the affected area. Fatty streaking is, of itself, of little significance. It is reversible and occurs naturally and temporarily in the arteries of young animals, particularly chicks but also mammals, including human babies. It can, however, be the forerunner of more serious atheromatous changes. When true atheroma develops, an area of the arterial wall becomes elevated so as to produce a 'signet ring' appearance. The elevation is due to an accumulation of fat and cholesterol, together with red blood cells and other inflammatory products, between the lining cells, the endothelium, and the internal elastic lamina. Abnormal cells also make their appearance in the swelling known as 'foam' cells, because of their foamy appearance; it appears that they have their origin in the smooth muscle cells, which become degenerated or altered in some other way; others say, however, that they are broken down 'lipophages' or fat-carrying cells, which have migrated in from the blood. The condition is worsened when, as eventually happens, the internal elastic lamina, dividing the internal coat from the middle coat, is disrupted and split; when this happens, cells and blood are forced from the middle coat into the atheroma and its size is greatly increased. In the long term, the plaque may become ulcerated and an aneurysm is likely to be formed; this is a pouch in the wall of the artery due to disintegration of the inner and middle coats. An aneurysm is a point of great weakness in an artery, which may become ruptured, causing haemorrhage, a common cause of stroke when this happens in a blood vessel in the brain. Alternatively, deposits of calcium may appear in the plaque, so that the wall of the artery becomes hard with lime salts.

Atheromatous plaques frequently become so large that they appear to block the entire lumen of the artery. Usually, however, the pulse of blood forces the plaque back into the artery wall and blood is able to flow without too much impediment. In this sense, the plaques are not by themselves a serious danger. It is, however, on these plaques that the intravascular thrombi form, and they can and do completely block affected arteries. Small deposits of fibrin, the material of blood clots, appear on the plaque and are progressively built up layer by layer to form the so-called 'luminal thrombus'. When this happens, an area of tissue supplied by the artery, usually of a wedge shape, dies for lack of oxygen and nutriment. Such areas lose the characteristic colour of the surrounding tissue and become white; they are thus easily detected and are known as 'infarcts'. The dead tissue is removed by the body's scavenging cells and is replaced by fibrous or scar tissue; meanwhile, new blood vessels are constructed to bypass the affected area by special cells known as 'angioblasts'. Coronary thrombosis results from a thrombus of this type in one of the coronary vessels, which supply the muscle of the heart, the 'myocardium'; the condition is known technically as a 'myocardial infarct'. A similar condition occurring in one of the cerebral arteries is known as a cerebral infarct; the result is a stroke, which can thus occur either from a thrombus or from haemorrhage arising from a ruptured aneurysm. Both myocardial and cerebral infarcts are dangerous and frequently fatal.

Such is the disease which is a major scourge of Westernised man living in civilised communities. I should, however, have written not disease but diseases, since there are two interrelated conditions involved, not necessarily due to the same causes; they therefore require to be studied independently of each other. Research, which has been on a massive and world-wide scale, has been concentrated more on the disease of the arteries than on the irrational clotting of the blood inside the arteries. It is supposed that, if the arteries can be maintained in health, then the blood clots will not occur. This view may well be mistaken: first, because it is probably a mistaken idea that arteries can ever be maintained throughout life in a healthy condition without a return to a more primitive way of life than would be acceptable; second, Russian workers have experimentally induced myocardial infarction in monkeys in the absence of both arterial disease and clotting; under conditions of severe stress, the coronary arteries have gone into a condition of spasm and the patient has died. Blockage of the artery may well, therefore, not be the sole cause of myocardial infarction. The development of spasm in a partially blocked artery could well account for the suddenness with which the condition frequently arises and for its association with conditions of great stress or strain.

Atheroma is almost universal in Westernised man, but almost unknown in non-Westernised peoples. It is virtually unknown in Arabs living their traditional lives, but in Arabs living in Israel, who have adopted a Western way of life, it is as frequent as it is in Israelis, and that is very frequent. In wild and domestic animals, myocardial infarction is a rare occurrence, though it has been described in both birds and mammals, especially primates. Atheroma, on the other hand, is by no means uncommon in certain groups of animals, and can be induced in experimental animals by feeding them diets high in saturated fats and cholesterol.

A massive review of the incidence of naturally occurring atherosclerosis in wild and domestic animals was made at a conference held in Los Angeles in 1964, to which 56 authors, all engaged in original research on the subject, contributed. The full proceedings were published under the editorship of James C. Roberts and Reuben Straus, who had convened the conference, in 1965. For the purpose of this review, I myself made a full analysis of all recorded cases of atherosclerosis and thrombosis in captive wild animals; other authors gave the results of their own work in different animal groups, both wild and domestic. The wide spread of animals that are affected by atherosclerosis is of great significance to the human problem and is worthy of brief analysis in relation to the present study. To quote from my own report:

It is our impression that, apart from the human species, the incidence of true atherosclerosis in mammals is low, though higher in birds. We find some correlation of incidence with age, but not with blood cholesterol levels. The incidence of atheroma in both mammals and birds is of interest owing to its virtual absence among certain groups. Among mammals, we find it primarily in primates (including man) and to a lesser extent among the Artiodactyla . . . In rodents, the condition is occasionally found among guinea pigs, chinchillas, rabbits and hares; it does not occur naturally in rats and mice but can be induced by experimental dietary means. Incidence is more widespread in birds, but here again it appears to be confined to certain groups and is virtually non-existent in others.

The susceptible groups of birds are then outlined, and in a later section of the report the following is stated:

The species distribution of atheroma susceptibility and insusceptibility suggests that nutrition may be the underlying factor in the development of the disease. Among birds, insusceptible species are those who feed normally on fruit or fresh animal food. Among mammals, the most susceptible group is the primates, including man. Man in his original state fed on a mixed diet with a high proportion of fruit and fresh animal protein. It may be suggested, therefore, that susceptible groups of animals are those whose natural diet would be fruit or fresh uncooked food of animal origin and who, under conditions of captivity, domestication or civilisation, are maintained on diets, in which grain predominates. The analogy holds good in respect of susceptible rodent family members, such as guinea pigs, chinchillas, and rabbits, who rely on fresh growing vegetable foods for their diet. Rats and mice on the other hand, naturally granivorous and adapted to life in sewers and ships and other places where fresh foods are not available, are atheroma insusceptible. The domestic pig, fed largely on an unnatural diet of grain, suffers from atheroma, while the wild pig, rooting for shoots and other germinating tuberous foods and killing rats and snakes as a fresh animal supplement, is rarely affected . . . We have supposed, therefore, that the development of atheroma in susceptible species may be primarily associated with enforced dietary habits of an unnatural nature. The main association appears to be with secondary granivorous habits, of which man himself, the greatest atheroma sufferer, is supremely guilty.

Herbert Ratcliffe, at one time director of the Penrose Institute at the Philadelphia Zoo, lends some support to these conclusions; he records that massive atheromata of the aorta and brachiocephalic arteries of the larger psittacine birds (macaws, cockatoos and parrots) usually disappear within two years when they are fed a high-quality mixed ration instead of sunflower seed. This observation is important in two respects: first, it shows that the lesions in the arteries are dependent on the diet given; second, that even massive atheromata can disappear if the diet is corrected. Evidence from Philadephia for animals other than psittacine birds is, however, somewhat contradictory. Feeding régimes for all but fish-eating animals were totally reformed in 1935 by the introduction of the well-known Ratcliffe diets, which have been the basis of animal feed formulas at many other zoos throughout the world. The Ratcliffe diets consist of formulated feeds, prepared at a central food kitchen to give a fully balanced diet supposedly satisfactory in all respects. Such régimes rely on some four formulations to feed all groups of animals; herbivorous, omnivorous, carnivorous and cage birds, each having their own formulation. In the ten years following the introduction of these feeds at Philadelphia, there was a marked increase in the incidence of atheroma in susceptible animal groups; in addition, the sites at which the atheromata developed shifted from the larger arteries, such as the aorta and brachiocephalic trunks, to smaller arteries such as the coronaries of the heart, and those of the kidneys. This change was attributed to factors of stress arising from increased population and crowding in the cages, together with ever-greater numbers of human visitors. The Ratcliffe diets are, however, largely composed of grain products, which, as seems likely, may be ill-tolerated by atheroma-susceptible species. The Philadelphia experience would appear to support this hypothesis. This is not to say that stress is not also involved, and indeed the monotony of the Ratcliffe diets might well contribute to it.

It is, however, clear that both domestic and captive wild animals are living in unnatural conditions, as is man himself, and to evaluate the situation evidence is required from animals living their natural lives in natural conditions. Do susceptible species, living in their natural environments, develop atheromatous lesions of their arteries at any stage of their existence? To answer this question is not so easy as might be supposed, because many animals living in the wild have become partially man-dependent, either scavenging his wastes or raiding his crops. However, with the aid of a grant from the British Heart Foundation, we mounted a three-year study to investigate it. A Cambridge honours graduate in zoology, Miss Sylvia Sikes, was employed; she was later awarded her Ph.D. on the results of her work, which is published in the *Transactions of the Zoological Society of London* (1969), vol. 32, part I. Dr Sikes' brief was to go to East Africa in order to study the incidence of arterial lesions, especially atheroma, in wild animals having regard to the distinction between those living in wild and disturbed habitats. Her studies give considerable insight into the problem of atherosclerosis and their significance has been widely overlooked.

There were two phases to the work: (1) a study of atheroma incidence in 43 species of free-living wild mammals and 25 species of birds; (2) a study of free-living wild elephants in three different habitat types—one natural and two 'stressed'. The elephant studies proved to be of the greatest importance as providing a significant comparison of wild animals in a natural habitat and two different kinds of disturbed habitat.

Sikes established in the first place that in both wild mammals and birds the deposition of lipid in the inner arterial walls, together with some thickening, commonly occurs and is natural and normal. The sites where this happens are at points of strain, mostly in the larger arteries, such as bifurcations or where tributaries are received. The thickenings thus have a supportive role and the lipid a cushioning effect. The frequency of lipid deposits was higher in birds than mammals; Sikes writes of them:

> Early fatty streaking and distinct fatty plaques in the aortic intima occurred in several of the specimens collected. They were most extensive in the ostriches and greater bustards. In no case was an advanced plaque seen, which could have had even a partially occlusive effect on the vessel.

In the mammals, apart from the physiological lipid deposits noted and the elephants described under, atheroma of the coronary arteries was found only in one specimen. This was from an elderly male chimpanzee shot on special licence in the Kigezi Game Reserve in Uganda. The chimpanzees in this area were the relics of a formerly larger population, which had declined because of inroads into the habitat by villages, tea plantations and lumbering activities. The chimpanzees were living, therefore, in stressed conditions and were not representative of what might happen in normal circumstances. In this elderly male, there were particularly occlusive atheromatous plaques in the coronary arteries and aorta comparable to those found in man. That such could occur in wild-living chimpanzees had previously been shown by the studies of two American scientists, Lindsay and Chaikoff, who reported that the only wild-living primates to suffer from atheroma were chimpanzees, South American spider monkeys, and some species of Asian macaques; it is not clear whether they too came from disturbed habitats, but this seems probable.

The elephant studies gave a clearer picture. In the undisturbed habitat, the Aberdare Mountain region of Kenya, there were found no abnormal conditions of arteries even in ageing elephants. These elephants were hunted from time to time, but otherwise were living the natural, normal lives of wild elephants. The other elephants studied came: first, from a scrubland habitat; and second, from a grassland habitat; both were de-generate habitats, over-populated with wildlife including elephants and showing vegetational changes. Elephants from both these habitats suf-fered from extensive and advanced arterial diseases in both large and small arteries, amongst which atheromatosis was prominent; however, the types of disease differed in prominence in the two habitats, but that need not concern us here. Dr Sikes attributed these changes both to de-privation of the elephants' natural diet and to stressing factors arising from the following: (1) prolonged exposure to unmitigated sunlight, because the trees had been destroyed; (2) over-population, which had occurred in spite of a diminution in the numbers born; (3) restricted diet; and (4) frustration of the migratory habit.

There have, of course, been other studies of arterial diseases in free-living wild animals, ranging from fish to whales, hippopotami and baboons, but none give the clear-cut answers of Sikes' study of elephants.

There has been much discussion as to whether lesions in animal arteries, whether experimentally induced or naturally occurring, are strictly com-parable to atheroma as it occurs in man. However, it seems reasonable to accept that lesions affecting the inner walls of arteries, which are morpho-logically similar and contain lipid substances, arise from similar causes and can justifiably be regarded as comparable. If so, we find ourselves with two main groups of factors which contribute to the development of atheroma: (1) nutritional; and (2) stress. To these, we should add a third, namely activity, since a healthy degree of exercise undoubtedly contributes to the avoidance of coronary episodes.

Coronary patients are often found to have excessive quantities of cholesterol in their blood. Cholesterol is, therefore, blamed for the con-dition and drugs are administered to reduce the level of cholesterol. Foods containing more than minimal amounts of cholesterol are also banned, including eggs. This reasoning is probably fallacious. Cholesterol is an important structural material in the body, being present in every body cell. The body itself manufactures cholesterol in the liver from simpler compounds; no animal can live without it. Eggs, though they certainly contain a significant quantity of cholesterol, also head the excellence league of foodstuffs both for amino acids and for unsaturated fats. These virtues surely outweigh the disadvantages of the cholesterol content; in any case, it is now coming to be accepted that it is not the cholesterol which is at fault, but deficiencies in the chemical products used to transport and distribute it around the body; these chemicals are the very proteins and unsaturated fatty acids in which eggs are rich. The body also has problems in transporting and breaking down saturated fats, when they are absorbed in excessive quantities; they too are deposited in fat depots and in the artery walls. It is known from numerous experiments that an excessive intake of cholesterol or saturated fats in the form of animal fats, including butter, causes atheroma. However, if these products are balanced in the diet with a sufficiency of unsaturated fats, atheroma is avoided. Both susceptible and insusceptible species of animals develop atheroma if sufficient saturated fat is added to the diet; still there is no reason to exclude butter, crispy bacon, and succulent joints from the diet, provided that the intake of animal fats is not excessively high and that it is balanced by a sensible intake of oily fats. Another school of thought blames sugar, of which we Westernised peoples consume large quantities in the form of sucrose or cane sugar.

The question of sugar is an interesting one in relation to the possibility of involvement of a diet high in grain products. Sucrose, so widely consumed in coffee, tea, cakes, sweets and puddings, is a disaccharide, or 12-carbon sugar composed of two monosaccharides or 6-carbon sugars; one of the monosaccharide units is glucose or dextrose, the other fructose (fruit sugar) or laevulose. These two sugars are often supposed to be mirror images of each other; this is incorrect, since although the one is right-handed in structure and the other left, the molecular design is different and chemically they behave differently, glucose as an aldehyde and fructose as a ketone. Metabolically these two sugars, which are separated during digestion, also behave in different ways. Glucose under the influence of insulin is built to a polysaccharide, glycogen or animal starch, and is stored in the liver and muscles. It is mobilised by adrenaline and, reconverted to glucose, powers all the muscles of the body, being broken down to carbon dioxide (CO_2) and water (H_2O) in the process. Glucose is present in blood, where its concentration is regulated within narrow limits; if the blood level falls below the danger limit, as in diabetics, unfortunate consequences follow, one being that fats cannot be fully broken down by oxidation and unpleasant and toxic substances, known as ketones, accumulate. The association with fat is of interest to our enquiry, and it is established that diabetics are more than normally susceptible to cardiac diseases.

Fructose, on the other hand, is used by the body in limited areas; it is for example the sugar present in semen and presumably plays a role in the nutrition of spermatazoa. It is sweeter than glucose and is the chief sugar present in fruits and in honey. In fruit-eating animals, which could include our remote ancestors, eating little fat it could be an important source of calories, hence the appeal of its sweet taste which we retain. Fructose, however, except as a source of calories, does not contribute to the body's energy systems. It is carried to the liver, and converted there to saturated fat. Milk sugar, lactose, is a disaccharide composed of two monosaccharides, glucose and galactose. The latter is presumably of especial value to the young animal and is present in the brain and other nervous tissues.

Grain foods contain a number of polysaccharides, that is complex starches, built up of sugars, of high molecular weight; they are not sweet, although built up of numerous monosaccharide units. The most important of these is starch proper, which is broken down in the course of digestion to the disaccharide maltose or malt sugar, which is constructed entirely of glucose units. Starch intake at levels required for caloric intake cannot, therefore, be a harmful food, and this could explain why primitive peoples, who only consume enough for their caloric requirements, do not build up excessive fat with deposits in their arteries. However, the problems of excessive starch intake in wealthy peoples and inadequate calorie intake in poor peoples have already been discussed in an earlier chapter. If starch is consumed in excess, the glucose derived from it will be largely converted into fat, some of which may be deposited in the arteries.

What then of stress? Can a chronic stressing situation, as with Dr Sikes' elephants, cause lipid to be deposited in arteries? Apart from actual nutritional defects, as considered above, inadequate or faulty diet is recognised to be amongst the major stressing factors, and so can operate in two ways through both metabolic and endocrine systems. This is perhaps best illustrated by the sad story of the Pacific Salmon, which suffer from widespread degenerative changes of the arteries, resembling atheroma, when journeying up rivers to spawn. The salmon are physically unable to feed, because their stomachs become blocked by tissue growth; yet they make journeys up to a thousand miles, spawn and die in a state of complete inanition. The calorie reserves of their bodies are mobilised to the maximum extent, in spite of which their livers become very fatty and widespread lesions develop in the inner coats of the arteries, including the coronaries. The fish are plainly in a state of stress, and suffer both from malnutrition and changes of function in the endocrine system. It may seem a far cry from spawning salmon to urbanised man, but the mechanisms involved are similar.

In spite of the high incidence of coronary thrombosis in young human males, the condition is rare in women until after the menopause, except when contraceptive pills are being taken; in this case, the incidence is slightly but significantly higher. Evidently, they are protected by one of the female sex hormones. Direct evidence of a link between stress and a slow accumulation of lipid in artery walls is not easy to obtain, but it has been shown in the chapter on stress that there are important alterations to blood flow patterns and pressures in this condition. Sikes has shown that lipid will physiologically be deposited in areas of artery walls, which are subjected to extra strain. It is known also from the work of J.E. Malcolm, now surgical consultant to the British Royal Air Force, that when flow patterns in arteries are altered or impeded, abnormal points of strain are created. Conditions, therefore, exist in which lipid deposits could well accumulate in arteries to the extent of becoming pathological, if there is long continued stress and feeding habits are such that excess lipid is present.

Man apart, intravascular clotting is extremely rare in the animal kingdom, though instances can be quoted, particularly in primates, both from my own experience and from the literature. Of itself, atherosclerosis can cause death in advanced age but is not dangerous in younger persons. Aged parrots are often found at autopsy with the condition so far advanced and the arteries so impregnated with calcium salts, that they snap like twigs. Why, then, is it that the arteries of Westernised human beings are so readily occluded by thrombi, when those of other animals are not, even if severely affected with atheromata? One would suppose that human blood was more liable to clot than that of other animals. To test this, a grant was obtained for a research worker in my department at the Nuffield Institute of Comparative Medicine to make comparative studies of the mechanism of clotting in man and other animals, wild and domestic. Dr Christine Hawkey was appointed to undertake this work, and over the years has produced results which have earned her a world-wide reputation. The factors involved in the clotting of blood are very complex, but in essence two major processes are involved. The first of these is the actual clotting; second, the mechanism by which a clot developed inside the body is destroyed again, known as 'thrombolysis'. Blood clots do form inside the body, when there has been tissue damage or haemorrhage, and they are the first stage in the repair process; they need to be removed when they have served their purpose so that repair or replacement of tissue can proceed. The small cells in the blood, known as platelets or thrombocytes, will adhere to a roughened surface in an artery, break down and release fibrinogen, the precursor of fibrin, the substance of the clot; other complex mechanisms then come into play to convert the fibrinogen into fibrin and the clot is started. Dr Hawkey's results showed that, contrary to expectation, human blood clotted far less readily than that of any other animals, including his cousin primates. Thrombolytic processes, on the other hand, were about the same. This result suggests that, from the circumstances of his life, man has been exposed to dangers from intravascular clotting for a very long time and that evolutionary processes have operated to protect him against it. As to what causes blood to clot inside the arteries in this unnatural manner, it is impossible to say. There is undoubtedly an association with stress, strain, anxiety and frustration, even excitement. Sometimes, coronary thrombosis or strokes develop slowly; equally often, they occur suddenly, when an individual about his or her normal affairs drops dead in a moment. Persons engaged in certain occupations succumb more readily than others. In many cases of unexplained crashes of air force single-seater fighter planes, it is found that the pilot, in his twenties, has succumbed to myocardial infarction. A survey was made at the London Hospital, in which it was found that the incidence of coronary thrombosis was higher in drivers of London buses than in conductors. This was attributed to the greater concentration and strain on the drivers, combined with less mobility. As I write these words on 17th August 1977, we hear of the death of Elvis Presley from a coronary episode at the age of 42. Here was a young man, who achieved the peak of fame, but had evident emotional problems; he has swelled the numbers of those cut off prematurely by this so-called senescent disease. Dr Hawkey in her studies found clear evidence that blood-clotting times were reduced under conditions of stress, and we can be sure that myocardial and cerebral infarction are closely associated with the stresses and strains of modern life.

Owing to the evident importance of stress in the causation of cardio-vascular disease, a paper summarising the position is added in the appendix. This was prepared by the author in 1972, but never published.

10 CANCER—IGNORANCE AND FEAR

Today, cancer is the second commonest cause of death amongst Western-ised peoples. It is also the most dreaded of all diseases to an extent that many, who fear they are afflicted, do not dare consult their doctors. As with cardio-vascular disease, one reason why cancer has become more prominent is the elimination of many infectious diseases as the cause of death; greater longevity will also increase the cancer incidence, where it is truly a disease of senescence. In spite of this, it seems that some forms of cancer are on the increase in a way that suggests a minor epidemic. The causes are not known, though many have been suggested. Such are the increase of radioactivity due to the use of X-rays in medicine, radioactive fall-out from nuclear explosions and power stations, and increased penetration of the ozone layer of the upper atmosphere by ultra-violet radiation. Another suggested cause is the use of industrial and agricultural chemicals, food additives and preservatives, cosmetics, drugs and other artificial substances in modern usage; indeed, there has been something of a witch-hunt for potentially carcinogenic materials in common use; even such old-established favourites as saccharin are being incriminated. Then there are such comforts of life as tobacco, which are said to ruin health and in particular to induce cancer. Finally, there are the undoubted hazards of certain occupations, such as silicosis in mine-workers and asbestosis in persons who work with asbestos.

Modern society is very much alive to these dangers and virtually everything possible is being done to prevent or avoid them, even when abandonment of certain products may result in great expense and cause great inconvenience. Even the removal of such avoidable causes of cancer appears to leave an unexplained increase in certain types, such as the leukaemias and breast cancer in women.

Significant advances have been made in the treatment of cancer and, provided that a case is reported and diagnosed early enough, many sufferers can be saved by surgery, drugs, ray treatments and so on. New techniques of early diagnosis have also been evolved, so that prospects for a patient have been greatly improved, and those who fear they may be affected do themselves a disservice if they do not consult their doctors. Nevertheless, there is little understanding of what cancer really is or what fundamentally causes it. One may reasonably ask what has become of the vast sums of money spent on cancer research since the beginning of the century, beyond the ability to halt the process in some patients in the early stages? As with other studies in this book, we shall look to the animal kingdom for our answers, and we shall find that the cause of many, perhaps most, animal cancers is known and that important advances have been made towards its prevention. It is inconceivable that the cause of similar animal cancers is different in man alone. Yet, the application of knowledge derived from such cancers in animals is proving extraordinarily difficult to apply to man, and scientists engaged in these studies are diffident about drawing conclusions from their results and in forecasting any early successful solution. The subject is of immense complexity, involving advanced techniques in virology, immunology and cytology. No adequate survey could be presented in a single chapter of a book. I shall, therefore, attempt to outline some of the fundamental problems and to show in what ways the increase in cancer incidence is yet another response to man's life in an unnatural environment.

In years gone by, students were taught that diseases could be classed in two groups, those that were inflammatory and those that were not inflammatory. Infectious diseases and injuries were accompanied by inflammation; cancers did not show signs of inflammation. The age-old definition of inflammation was: 'rubor, dolor, tumor, turgor', redness, pain, swelling and tumescence. Cancers were tumours, but redness, pain and tumescence were absent. Tumours could be benign or malignant. Benign tumours grow to a certain extent, then cease to grow and do not spread. The true cancer, or neoplasm, continues to grow at the expense of the tissue in which it is located and neoplastic cells may be carried in the blood or lymph vessels to new sites, where they start secondary cancers or 'metastases'. In this way, cancers can spread to many vital organs, leading to a slow and agonising death. There are many different kinds of cancers, which receive names indicating the kind of tissue in which they originate; thus, a chondroma is a cancer originating in cartilage, an osteoma in bone, a lymphoma in lymph tissue, an adenoma in gland tissue, and so on. There occur also mixed cancers, such as a fibrosarcoma, a cancer of fibrous tissue and connective tissue. Often, cancers are difficult to identify and experts may disagree as to the type. It is, however, important to identify them, since different tumours behave in different ways and have different characteristics; a lymphoma is a rapidly progressive eroding tumour which eats through the tissues and rapidly kills the patient; other cancers progress more slowly, but no less insidiously. The leukaemias are a group of cancers which affect the parent cells of the red or white blood corpuscles leading to a progressively fatal anaemia.

Cancer cells have undergone a mutation, from which they have acquired special properties. The growth and division rates of normal cells are regulated by restraints imposed by chemicals produced in the tissue which ensure orderly growth and replacement of cells as needed. Cancer cells are not subject to these restraints, and so continue unfettered growth and division at the expense of normal cells. Actually, they divide much more slowly than normal cells, but since they grow and divide continuously they outstrip those of the tissue and replace them. They can also grow and divide in the absence of oxygen, which is essential for normal cells. There has clearly been genetic change, and many workers believe that the one indispensable element in cancer may be a virus or its genetic material. Cancer cells seem to have a new genetic input that allows them to make new and unique antigens. Carcinogenic chemicals and physical agents, such as radiation, do not provide such input; they only rearrange the output. It is believed that throughout life the body's tissues are continually producing 'rogue' cells, but that they are normally identified as foreign bodies and destroyed by the immune defences. Thus some interference with the body's immunity system is involved in the development of cancers, as for instance if they are depressed by other diseases or in conditions of stress or depression. Furthermore, if viral infections are involved, then the body's immunity systems would also be active in controlling the virus also. The possibility of virus involvement may now engage our attention.

The involvement of viruses in animal cancers appears to be widely unknown or ignored. I had occasion to write a letter to the Editor of *New Scientist*, protesting at the apparent indifference of British scientists to progress that had been made. This was dated 6 December 1976 and was duly published. The following is an extract:

We know today that a great many animal cancers—perhaps all—from frogs to higher primates are caused by viral infections, leukaemias, lymphomas, sarcomas, and carcinomas. We know the main viral groups involved, Herpes, Papova, and Oncorna B & C. We know that most animal cells, including human, harbour potentially oncogenic viruses in their genetic material. We know that these viruses are handed down vertically from mother to offspring, including human. We know that these viruses, under certain circumstances such as exposure to oncogenic chemicals—co-factors—, cause mutagenic changes in cells. We know that these viruses, by their own means of genetic engineering, displace a segment of host DNA and substitute their own genes. We know that RNA viruses can make DNA replicas of themselves by means of their enzyme 'reverse transcriptase', and that they then behave in the same way. Furthermore, we know that oncogenic viruses can also spread horizontally from one infected animal to another that is not infected. We know also that inside cells some of these viruses, notably the oncorna group, can hybridise with different strains, so that new antigenic sub-types can readily appear, as with influenza.

I then go on to point out that a vaccine is already on the market, which protects fowls from a lymphoid cancer, known as Marek's Disease, and that experimentally anti-leukaemia vaccines have been successful in marmosets, which are small monkeys. This letter, given a prominent position in *New Scientist* and first in the correspondence columns, was greeted with deafening silence, no correspondent writing either to agree or disagree. The points made, I shall now elaborate.

The knowledge that some animal cancers are caused by viruses is by no means new. In 1908, two Danish scientists, Wilhelm Ellerman, a veterinary surgeon, and Olaf Bang, a doctor, transmitted experimentally a form of fowl leukaemia from fowl to fowl by means of filtered material that contained no tissue cells or bacteria, that is material that could contain no infectious agent except a virus. In 1910, an American scientist, Peyton Rous, transmitted another tumour of fowls, now known as the Rous Sarcoma, between fowls also using cell-free material, hence establishing that the cancers were caused by a virus. Marek's Disease of chickens was also proved to be caused by a virus by another American scientist, Pappenheimer, in 1926. In 1933, the important and serious group of diseases known as chicken lymphomatosis, was shown by another American scientist, Jacob Furth, to be also due to filterable virus infection.

In 1936 came an important advance, when John J. Bittner at the Jackson Memorial Laboratory in Bar, Maine, showed that the mammary carcinoma of mice is transmitted by a filterable infectious agent in the milk; the young mice acquire infection when suckling and develop tumours when adult. The importance of this discovery can be gauged by the following quotation from the 1976 report of the US National Cancer Institute on the 'Virus Cancer Program' (the programme incidentally was funded during the year at the staggering figure of $63,000,000): 'Indirect evidence continues to accumulate that there are entities in human milk and breast tumours that are structurally, immunologically, and genetically similar to mouse mammary tumour virus (MMTV).'

In 1938, a kidney tumour of frogs was shown by Baldwin Lucké of Philadelphia to be caused by a virus. The tumour is a renal carcinoma

and the virus came to be known as the Lucké virus. The search has now
widened from chicks to frogs and mice, and in 1951 it was shown by
Ludwic Gross that leukaemia of mice was also caused by a filterable
virus and that the same virus could also cause leukaemia in rats. This
investigator in 1953 recovered another virus from tumours of parotid
glands in mice. He found further, that this same virus, when injected
into new-born mice, caused also subcutaneous sarcomas, carcinomas of
the mammary glands, and tumours of the medullary portions of the
adrenal glands. This virus was further investigated by two workers,
Stewart and Eddy, at the National Institute of Health. They renamed
the virus 'polyoma virus', and succeeded in propagating it in tissue
cultures of embryonic mouse cells. For the first time, a carcinogenic
virus had been grown outside a living body; furthermore, in culture it
developed infective properties also for rats and hamsters, showing that
this virus at any rate is malleable and can alter its properties. In 1957,
a further oncogenic virus of mice was found by Charlotte Friend at the
Sloan-Kettering Institute in New York.

Eddy and her co-workers at the National Institute of Health contributed a further important advance in 1961 and 1962, the same discovery also being made by Girardi in 1962 and his colleagues working
at the Merck Institute in West Point, Pennsylvania. These workers were
studying a virus known as SV40 (simian virus 40). This virus was proving
troublesome, because it appeared spontaneously in cultures of rhesus
monkey kidney cells used in the manufacture of adeno-virus vaccine.
To everybody's dismay and astonishment, it was found to cause progressive sarcomas in new-born hamsters—dismay because it had been thought
harmless and had been incorporated in some batches of adeno-virus
vaccine. A similar virus has more recently been isolated from human
tissues, which may be associated with some forms of human cancer. The
discovery was disturbing for a further reason, namely, that a virus had
now been isolated from one of man's cousin primates, which possessed
oncogenic properties. The trail of investigation is coming nearer to the
human species and came nearer still in 1962, when Trentin and his colleagues at Baylor University in Houston showed that a specifically human
virus, known as adeno-virus 12, also induced sarcomas in new-born hamsters; several other human adeno-viruses have also been shown subsequently to be potentially oncogenic. In 1964, Jarrett and his colleagues,
working at the Glasgow Veterinary School, showed that leukaemia of
cats too was caused by a filterable virus. Since that time, the leukaemias
of cattle, dogs and guinea pigs have also proved to be of infectious origin,
and Russian workers have isolated a virus which causes leukaemia in

macaque monkeys and baboons. Viruses have also been found to be the cause of many other tumours of animals, including monkeys.

During the course of these studies, another myth was laid to rest. It was conceded that some few cancers of animals might be caused by virus infections, but viruses—it was supposed—were just one of a number of irritant agents, which stimulated tissue cells to become carcinogenic. A sense of comfort was derived from the belief that these viruses were specific to a single host and could not infect, let alone cause cancer in, others. This happy belief was shattered in respect of virtually all the viruses studied. Let us consider, for example, the Rous Sarcoma Virus of chickens. The first blow to existing beliefs came when it was shown that chicken tumours induced by carcinogenic chemicals later produced the Rous Virus in recoverable quantities. The chemicals, therefore, did not *cause* the cancer; they merely activated a virus that was latent. It was then found that, though the Rous Virus causes tumours, it is unable to propagate itself unless a second virus is also present, known as a 'helper' virus; more than one virus may, therefore, be involved in cancer etiology, making the study that much more difficult. The Rous Virus was then found to cause tumours also in ducks, pheasants, turkeys and pigeons; so much for the specificity theory of carcinogenic viruses, which was to reel from further blows. A number of different strains or sub-types of Rous Virus appeared in the hands of different investigators, each with somewhat different properties, each being capable of infecting different animals. In total, using all these different strains, cancers can be caused by this virus in rats and mice, hamsters, guinea pigs, dogs and monkeys. The leukaemias of mice have been extensively studied, and all types have been shown to be caused by filterable viruses; even when induced by radiation, infective viruses can be isolated, showing that the effect of radiation is to activate the virus, not to cause cancer.

A further advance of highest importance occurred when Melendez and a group of workers at the New England Primate Center at Southborough, Massachusetts, isolated a new herpesvirus from squirrel monkeys. The virus was isolated in 1968 and named *Herpesvirus saimiri*. In 1970, Melendez and his colleagues reported that this virus was carried as a latent pathogen in squirrel monkeys, but when transferred to marmosets or owl monkeys caused malignant lymphoma or acute lymphocytic leukaemia. In 1972, the same group of workers found another oncogenic herpesvirus in spider monkeys, which caused leukaemia in marmosets; this was named *Herpesvirus ateles*.

The proof that herpesviruses from primates can cause cancer was of great importance to students of human cancers, since viruses of this group were already suspect as the cause of two human cancers. Carcinoma of the cervix in women is commonly associated with the presence of *Herpesvirus simplex* type 2 and is believed to be a venereal disease, the virus being acquired from the male partner. The second suspect occurs in the so-called Burkitt Lymphoma, a malignant lymphoma of African children first investigated by a British surgeon, Dennis Burkitt, in Uganda in 1962 and 1963. A virus is commonly associated with these cases and was isolated by Anthony Epstein, now Professor of Pathology at the Bristol (England) University Medical School. This virus has been named Epstein-Barr Virus (EBV) and in temperate climates is the cause of glandular fever (Infectious Mononucleosis); it has also been suggested as the cause of naso-pharyngeal carcinoma in man. In Africa and other tropical countries, distribution of the Burkitt Lymphoma coincides with endemic malaria areas, and it has been suggested that malaria infection is the co-factor which causes the virus to become oncogenic. EBV is a herpesvirus. *H. simplex*—2, the possible cause of cervical carcinoma, causes herpetic lesions on the genitalia of human males and females; it is venereally transmitted.

While a great many, if not most, animal cancers are now known to be caused by infectious agents, definite proof of the involvement of such in human cancers is still awaited. Although it seems impossible that only human cancers do not have an infectious origin, there are still many sceptics and indeed the final proof is extremely elusive. Even so, there exists a strong body of circumstantial evidence that human cancers are also infectious. While cancers are mostly of sporadic occurrence, this is not always so. There are many instances in which a particular cancer has run in families. While this may suggest a genetic influence, it also suggests that vertical transmission of an oncogenic virus has occurred from mother to child. There is evidence, also, that leukaemia sometimes occurs in 'clusters' in children attending the same school or living in the same small community; this evidence would suggest horizontal transmission from one child to another, but is not sufficiently strong to be significant. There is, however, abundant evidence, as from surgeons operating on cancer patients, that human cancers can be transferred from one person to another. To prove the viral etiology of such transmissions would require that such transmissions should be effected by material free from cancer cells, which would entail the deliberate use of human beings as experimental animals. Such experiments could be undertaken on dying patients, if the recipient consented; however, it may take some years for a cancer to develop, so little advantage would be gained. There have been a few attempts to transmit human cancers in volunteers, but the results have been inconclusive. Numerous attempts have been made to transmit human cancers to animals, from mice to monkeys, and some have been apparently successful. However, the scientific fraternity remains to be convinced; it is usually objected that the human material may have induced the activity of an oncogenic virus latent in the experimental animals.

The argument that, when monkeys are injected with material from human cases of leukaemia, they develop monkey leukaemia and not human leukaemia may seem somewhat specious, but there are reasons for supposing that this may happen, and scientists are right to be sceptical. However, the evidence for viral involvement in human cancers is reinforced in other ways. In blood from leukaemic patients, and in tumour tissues, virus particles identical with those which cause similar diseases in animals can be detected by electron microscopy and similar viruses can be recovered in tissue cultures by sophisticated techniques. Furthermore, by immunity tests on blood serum, it is found that patients possess immune bodies to these viruses. Neither the viruses nor the immune bodies can be demonstrated in unaffected persons, though a reservation must be made to this statement, which will be discussed under. Many a criminal has been convicted on more slender evidence than implicates viral infections as the cause of human cancers. The evidence is convincing, but does not constitute positive scientific proof. The difficulty lies in the complicated interactions between three variable factors: (1) the viruses and their modes of behaviour; (2) the body's tissue cells and these viruses; and (3) the response of the body's immunity systems to (a) the viruses and (b) the cancer cells themselves.

There are at least five groups of viruses involved in the causation of cancer: (1) the herpesvirus group; (2) the oncornavirus group, associated with many of the common cancers, the leukaemias, lymphomas, sarcomas and carcinomas; (3) the adenovirus group; (4) the papovavirus group; and (5) the poxvirus group. Many of these viruses cause transitory and inapparent illness in their natural hosts, febrile diseases in some animals, and cancer in others. They may, indeed, cause one type of disease in the young of the species, and cancer in older animals. From this, it is evident that it is not the property of any one group of viruses to cause cancer but the interaction of the viruses with the host's cells and immunity systems. All viruses must live and multiply inside the host's cells; they are incomplete forms of life, and cannot like bacteria live in the tissues or body fluids. They possess either DNA or RNA, never both, though both are essential to living systems. To multiply, therefore, they must manipulate the host DNA, forcing it to produce the proteins needed to manufacture more virus particles. Those viruses, which possess DNA only but no RNA, such as the herpesviruses, directly enter the host cell nucleus, shedding their protein coat in the process. RNA viruses, on the other hand, such as the oncornaviruses, would normally live and replicate in the cell cytoplasm. However, they possess an enzyme, a polymerase known as 'reverse transcriptase', by which they make DNA copies of themselves, which can enter the host nucleus as do the DNA viruses. When the virus particles—or genomes—enter the nucleus of the host cell, they cause a portion of the host DNA thread—the genetic material—to break away and they insert their genome in its place. The host cell mostly continues to code for its normal functions, but also to produce more virus particles. It is not necessarily damaged; any abnormal cells produced as a result are destroyed by the immunity systems, which also check the virus from assuming control. For the cells of the tissue to be changed into cancer cells requires one or more of certain conditions; dominance of the virus may be stimulated by a co-factor, such as radiation or a carcinogenic chemical; suppression of the immune factors which keep the virus in check; or the presence of a 'helper' virus.

The demonstration of viruses in cancers has presented great difficulty, although immune reactions to them can be measured and particles resembling viruses can be seen under the electron microscope. The difficulty lies in the isolation of viruses in tissue culture, so that their properties and pathogenic potential can be studied. In humans, although experiments to transmit disease to other humans are precluded, the viruses could be grown with healthy human cells in tissue cultures, both with and without cancer-inducing co-factors, to determine whether they are converted to cancer cells. In tumours, free virus is present and can be cultured, though with difficulty; in healthy cells, there is no free virus and until recently means did not exist, whereby the presence of virus in the host genome could be demonstrated. However, simple and ingenious means have now been discovered, whereby this can be done. If cells carrying a passenger virus are cultured on their own, the presence of virus cannot be demonstrated. If, however, such cells are grown in culture together with cells of a related animal species, which are susceptible of penetration by the virus, the virus will appear in the related cells causing cytopathogenic changes, and it can be recovered from them. Use of this technique has produced surprising results. It has been found that most, if not all, animal cells, including human, carry potentially oncogenic viruses as passengers in the genome. Viruses carried are especially the C type oncornaviruses, responsible in animals for leukaemias, lymphomas, sarcomas and carcinomas. The presence of these viruses can be demonstrated in the placenta, the foetus and the newborn, including human babies.

Cancers associated with viruses could, therefore, arise in at least four ways. First, they could arise if cells carrying virus were assaulted by carcinogenic influences, especially if the immune system were depressed by infection or anxiety. Second, they could arise if the host became additionally infected with a 'helper' virus. Third, they could arise from horizontal infection by a carcinogenic virus, either from a human or animal source, to which there was inadequate resistance. Fourth, they could arise if a new virus was horizontally acquired, which hybridised with a resident virus. These possibilities are being very actively explored at the present time, and to this student of the subject it would appear that favourable results must be achieved in the near future. The complexities are, however, so great, that many scientists actively engaged in research on the subject are less sanguine, though most agree that the cancer problem will be resolved within the next ten to twenty years. The strange ways in which these viruses react with each other is well illustrated by the story of the vaccine prepared against Marek's Disease of poultry, the only anti-cancer vaccine so far to be in commercial production.

The vaccine against Marek's Disease, a cancer of lymphoid tissues of poultry, is a live viral vaccine and is very effective in protecting poultry against the disease. The virus involved is a B type herpesvirus. The virus used to make the vaccine is a herpesvirus of turkeys, which does not cause either disease or tumours in poultry, although it is closely related to the virus of Marek's Disease. The vaccine virus is given to day-old chicks; it establishes a latent infection, which lasts for the life of the bird. The virus does *not* prevent the bird from becoming infected with the virus of Marek's Disease. It does prevent the Marek's virus from causing cancer. The mechanism by which this result is obtained is unknown, but a complex interaction between virus, cell and immunity systems is suggested. If, as seems certain, the development of some, if not all, cancers requires the presence of a virus in the host genome, it must in time be possible to devise means such as this to protect potential sufferers at least against those which most commonly occur.

In Britain today, both in lay and medical circles, there is an air of profound gloom about the cancer situation. So many people, in early and middle age, die lingering and agonising deaths in spite of surgical, ray and drug treatments, which of themselves cause acute distress. Hopes were aroused when drugs were found that would suppress some cancers, and indeed their use in childhood leukaemias has been effective and valuable. In other cancers, results have been disappointing. It is of little comfort to cancer patients that there are good grounds for supposing that a solution to the problem may be imminent. To the general population, concerned for the well-being of sons and daughters and grand-children, the outlook can bring hope and confidence, especially to families in which there have been cancer deaths.

For the purpose of this book, I am suggesting that the alarming increase in cancer cases is yet another result of man's response to his unnatural urbanised environment. It is no doubt in part associated with greater longevity, but this is only part of the explanation. What new threats will emerge, when the alleged diseases of senescence—cancer and cardio-vascular disease—have been overcome, belongs to the history of man's future.

INFLATING THE BALLOON

When some clever person invents some useful gadget, such as a polished stone axe, a new flint arrow head, a chariot, an aeroplane, or a television set, he causes inflation. If people are to acquire these things, more resources must be created, and more manpower diverted from producing the primary necessities of life; new flint mines must be opened, and a specialist class must come into being to work the flint and to distribute it. The whole of civilisation, from flint to rocket, from Stone to Space Age, is a tale of inflation, the spawn of inventiveness. Man's lot can only be improved by invention, and the necessity of invention is revealed in man's struggle to adapt himself to the problems of life in urbanised societies. Once started, inflation must inexorably continue, if life is to be happy and comfortable. The achievements of medical science, which have brought such spectacular improvements in health and life expectancy, have themselves been bought at the cost of inflation.

Inflation is to be deprecated only when it outstrips resources, which at intervals in human history it has invariably done. Man is like a child inflating balloons before a party. The child blows and inflates the balloon, until he comes to the end of his breath; the balloon partly deflates and he blows some more; the process is repeated until the balloon is filled. Indications are that man's balloon is nearly full. What will he do when it is full? He may loose his grip, and the balloon will deflate again. He may tie it off, as the child hopes to do, and so achieve equilibrium. Or, he may go on blowing, until it bursts with a big bang in which he and his little world will be destroyed.

The achievement of equilibrium is the basis of many philosophies. The Christian aspires to a new life in heaven, where all that is good will live to eternity in equilibrium with the heavenly father, all that is bad being eternally consumed in hell fire. The Buddhist achieves perfection through multiple lives, and will then live in equilibrium in the eternal peace of nirvana. Man aspires to escape from the struggles of his inflationary existence; perhaps he was happier in the old Stone Age, when he was part of a stable ecological unit of the environment. However, those days are long since past. Man must inflate or die, but what will happen to him when inflation reaches the maximum which earthly resources can permit? In theory, Marxism provides the answer; a classless society will be achieved, in which all accept equality, and the rule of law and the processes of government become of secondary importance. No doubt, many Marxists believe that this can be achieved; many others would plainly like a classless and docile proletariat, but would include themselves in a privileged ruling elite—hardly the recipe we are seeking. Nor are Marxist governments more obviously dedicated to equality between nations; they appear more concerned with the imminent shortage of energy sources, food and raw materials, being poised to grab what remains, when the right time comes. If they are successful, the balloon will again deflate; if challenged, the big bang could result.

We have supposed that man's inventive restlessness has been the result of frustrated nomadism. Can such a creature ever adopt a docile and submissive existence through countless generations in an urbanised society? Who would not rather be one of George Orwell's proles, living in squalor and freedom, than belong to his classless society of robots? Are not ideas of heaven, nirvana, and the classless society illusions, just as the tired businessman dreams of living in bliss in the countryside, smoking his pipe, and poking fat pigs with his stick? Man must be eternally on the move, if not physically, then intellectually. If so, then the problem remains as to what happens when he has inflated himself to the limits of the earth's resources? On the face of it, deflation would appear to be the only answer; however, the question is worthy of examination.

One thing is certain, that the world of our grandchildren or great-grandchildren in a hundred years time will be very different from that in which we live today, but its shape and form will be determined by our actions now. How comfortable and satisfying will be their lives will depend greatly on how many of them there are. There is only one humane and effective way of controlling population numbers; that is to give people the desire and incentive to limit family size by making them prosperous. People living at subsistence level with a short life expectation have no incentive to limit family numbers and so, with the aid of advanced medical science, population numbers increase. Where there is a choice between spending money on large families, or having a more comfortable life, better food, buying more personal possessions, and giving greater educational and other advantages to fewer children, nine times out of ten family numbers are voluntarily limited. Two questions are begged: first, that those who control resources are prepared to share them; and second, that adequate resources are available. Sharing of resources does not mean that a minority of people are concerned with development and production, handing over the products of their skills and industry without return; it means that assistance must be given to those people who are at subsistence level to produce what is necessary for life and trade,

and to buy from them what they wish to sell at prices which will en-
hance their standards of life. This approach will of itself increase
resources. What of the resources themselves? Have we already reached
a stage when decline is inevitable because they are simply not adequate
for the purpose? Unless the world's resources of energy and raw materials have been grossly underestimated, evidently time is very short, but
possibly still adequate to match them to the requirement of providing
adequate standards of life to encourage limitations of family size.

Food is the product of solar radiation and fertile soil. Solar radiation
is income, and not capital; hard as we may try, we cannot squander it.
We can, on the other hand, destroy the fertility of soil, and indeed man
has been singularly adept at doing so from Roman times onwards. However, the fertility of soils can be maintained and improved by proper
management, and we know today very well how this can be done. There
would appear, therefore, to be no insuperable problem over matching
requirements of food and other products grown in soils to requirements.

Where capital, as opposed to income, resources are involved, the situation is very different. Without the capital resources of energy and raw
materials that man acquires from fossil sources, life as he has engineered
it cannot continue for very much longer. In this sense, life in the days of
our great-grandchildren is likely to be much impoverished, even if a
global struggle for these resources has not destroyed them. The exhaustion of oil reserves within a hundred years had been predicted at least
forty years ago. Yet nothing was done, and both oil and other minerals
have been squandered at such a rate that time in which to develop alternatives may now be inadequate. Alternatives to metals are themselves
produced from coal and oil, as are the drugs on which our health programmes depend; but their production needs energy also, and this means
more coal and oil to produce the fabric of our machines and our chemicals. Plainly coal and oil should be conserved for manufactures, until
such time as the excess carbon reserves in the atmosphere and abundant
materials such as silica can be harnessed for the purpose. We desperately
require alternative sources of energy.

Even at this late hour, this can no doubt be achieved, especially if use
is made of nuclear fuels to bridge an awkward time gap. Income sources
of power and energy available on earth are more than adequate for man's
purposes. Such are powered by solar and lunar energy, the winds, the
waves, the tides and direct solar power. Abundant energy is locked in chemical compounds, such as hydrogen, though its release poses technical problems of great difficulty. As with food, then, there appear to be no problems
that are insuperable, but they will not be solved unless all of mankind can

work together towards their solution, and unless incentives are provided to encourage limitation of families. The omens are not unhopeful, but problems past and present must be understood and old enmities buried.

APPENDIX: STRESS AND CARDIO-VASCULAR DISEASE

It is widely believed that stress, either physical or mental, can initiate coronary episodes, though little attention appears to be paid to this aspect of the subject. This contribution briefly reviews the literature and suggests areas in which stress may be important.

(1) Coronary Insufficiency in Stressed Monkeys

Lapin and Yakovleva (1963) point out that coronary insufficiency in monkeys is frequently associated with hypertension, both being somatic manifestations of a neurosis. The condition may lead to cardio-sclerosis, which sometimes occurs also in the absence of hypertension. Athero-sclerosis is usually absent.

Experiments are described in which 'conflict' type neuroses of Pav-lovian type were induced in monkeys and led to hypertension and cor-onary insufficiency. Many of the monkeys survived these derangements for up to six years. One monkey died from cerebral haemorrhage. Renal lesions, particularly of the glomeruli, were also found.

In Fiennes (ed.) (1966), further information is given on the subject by Lapin, Yakovleva and Cherkovich, and it is here stated that both coronary insufficiency and hypertension follow exposure of baboons to natural neurotising situations and that myocardial infarction—in the absence of atheroma of the coronaries—may result.

(2) Stress and Metabolism

A relationship between stress and cholesterol levels in the blood and arterial walls has been demonstrated by a number of workers, mostly in rats. A recent paper by C.M. Lang (1967) describes work on squirrel monkeys (*Saimiri sciureus*). Two groups were subjected to intermittent stress over a period of 25 months, consisting of (a) restraint plus electric shock with executive control; (b) restraint alone; and (c) a control group. Results in the two experimental groups were similar and showed: (i) the mean serum cholesterol was higher following the period of stress; (ii) the excretion of urinary 17-ketosteroids was increased; (iii) coronary artery atherosclerosis was more marked; (iv) ECG changes were present in some of the test monkeys; (v) no weight changes occurred in the adrenal glands but histological changes were observed; (vi) increase in blood lipids was less than that of lipids in the coronary musculature.

S.N. Jagannathan *et al.* (1964), however, found that long-term administration of adrenaline caused focal intimal changes in the aortas of monkeys (*Macaca radiata*), with accumulation of neutral fat and mucopolysaccharides. These monkeys suffered a substantial fall of serum cholesterol at the end of two weeks, which remained during the experiment. Hepatic cholesterol and lipid content were unaltered.

Maier *et al.* (1963) recorded a reduction of serum cholesterol, both free and esterified, in stressed rhesus monkeys. In males, the fall was 35.5 per cent; in females only 19.0 per cent. After the experiment, the males returned to normal, but serum cholesterol of the females rose to figures significantly above normal. The authors believe that the hypothalamus controls circulating lipids and even the induction of atherogenesis.

The effects of stress on cholesterol metabolism, then, appears to be variable and requires to be studied.

(3) Stress and Atherosclerosis

Lang, quoted in the last section, showed that the degree of atherosclerosis in squirrel monkeys subjected to intermittent stress was higher than in controls.

Ratcliffe and Cronin (1958) and Ratcliffe, Yerasimides and Elliott (1960) record studies on animals at the Philadelphia Zoo, in which it is claimed that there was an increased incidence of atheroma in the arteries of the zoo animals during two decades after larger numbers were kept in the cages, in spite of an improvement to the animals' diets. The increase in mammals was ten-fold and in birds twenty-fold. Lesions tended also to be found in new sites, namely the distal, intramural segments of the coronary arteries occurring as intimal thickenings and occlusion. There have also been instances of myocardial infarction and sudden death in both mammals and birds. Ratcliffe and Snyder (1964) demonstrated a relationship between the social grouping of white leghorn chickens and the occurrence of myocardial infarcts.

Sikes (1969) has shown that wild-living elephants in stressed habitats suffer from atherosclerosis, while those in unstressed habitats do not. Amongst other factors involved, she believes that lack of shade leads to frustrating conditions and stress.

(4) Stress and Blood Clotting

There is evidence also that clotting times are reduced in stressed animals. For instance, Cannon and Mildenhall (1914) showed that in cats exposed to stress, clotting times were shortened and that the same effect could be produced by injections of adrenaline. Other evidence appears to come entirely from humans, e.g. Dreyfuss (1956), Forewell and Ingram (1957), Ogston *et al.* (1962) and Innes and Sevitt (1964). These workers made observations on persons receiving adrenaline injections and exposed to stressing situations, e.g. before examinations, about to take part in laboratory tests or following severe injury. In these subjects, too, clotting times were reduced.

(5) Stress and Fibrinolysis

Both Ogston and Innes and Sevitt showed that, while clotting times were shortened in stressing conditions, fibrinolytic activity increased. The effects of stress on fibrinolysis, however, appear to be somewhat variable and more evidence is required; the subject is reviewed by Fearnley (1965).

(6) Stress and Platelet Adhesiveness

There appears to be no evidence as to the effect of stress on platelet stickiness. Dr Hawkey has drawn my attention to two papers on the effects of adrenaline, and of adrenaline and ADP on platelet stickiness, those of Besterman *et al.* (1967) and of Macmillan (1966).

From these, it appears that adrenaline increases platelet stickiness both *in vivo* and *in vitro*. It also potentiates ADP-induced platelet aggregation by stimulating release of ADP from the platelets themselves.

(7) Stress and Vascular Endothelium

There is one title available on the subject of stress effects on vascular endothelium, that of A.A. Katzberg on 'Stress induced fragility of adrenal sinusoids in the baboon'. Anaesthetised baboons were subjected to stress by rapid deceleration, during which they encountered forces from 20 to 30 Gs. Zones of haemorrhage of the sinusoids occurred in the outer half of the *Zona fasciculata* and adjacent to the *Zona glomerulosa*. The damage is regarded as being due to stress and not of haemodynamic origin.

Conclusion

It appears that the effects of stress are divisible in relation to a number of factors, known to be associated with atherosclerosis, hypertension and coronary episodes. Its effect is potentially important, but too little information exists as yet to assess this.

References

Besterman, E. *et al.* (1967). Diurnal Variations of Platelet Stickiness compared with Effects Produced by Adrenaline. Brit. Med. J., 1967, *1*, 597-600

Cannon, W.B. and Mendenhall, W.L. (1914). Adrenaline injection shown to shorten clotting time in cats. *Am. J. Physiol, 34,* 255

Dreyfuss, F. (1956). Clotting time in normal humans shortened before examinations and at times of increased occupational stress. *J. Psychosom. Res., 1,* 252 (Friedman *et al.* (1958), *Circulation, 17,* 852)

Fearnley, G.R. (1965). *Fibrinolysis,* pp. 17 and 46. London: Arnold.

Forewell, D. and Ingram, G.I. (1957). Infusion of Adrenaline to humans shortens clotting time. Causes increase in factor V or factor VIII. *J. Physiol., 135,* 370-83

Innes, D. and Sevitt, S. (1964). Shortened clotting time and increased fibrinolytic activity in severely injured patients. *J. Clin. Path., 17,* 1

Jagannathan, S.N. *et al.* (1964). Effect of adrenaline on aortic structure and serum cholesterol in *Macaca radiata. J. Atherosch. Res., 4,* 335

Katzberg, A.A. (1968). Stress induced fragility of adrenal sinusoids in the baboon. *Anat. Rec., 160,* 479 (Abstract only)

Lang, C.M. (1967). Effects of psychic stress on atherosclerosis in the Squirrel Monkey *(Saimiri sciureus). Proc. Soc. exp-Biol.* (N.Y.), *126,* 30-4

Lapin, B.A. and Yakovleva, L.A. (1963). *Comparative Pathology in Monkeys.* Springfield, Ill.: Thomas

Lapin, B.A., Yakovleva, L.A. and Cherkovich, G.M. (1966). Use of non-human primates in Medical Research, Especially in the study of Cardio-vascular Pathology and Oncology. In *Some Recent Developments in Comparative Medicine,* ed. R.N.T.-W.-Fiennes, pp. 195-212. *Symp. zool. Soc. Lond.,* No. 17. London, Academic Press

Macmillan, D.C. (1966). Secondary clumping effect in human citrated platelet-rich plasma produced by adenosine diphosphate and adren-aline. *Nature, 211,* No. 5045, pp. 140-4, 9 July 1966

Meier, R.M. *et al.* (1963). Sex differences in the serum cholesterol response to stress in Monkeys. *Nature, 199,* 812

Ogston, D. *et al.* (1962). Shortening of calcium clotting time and increased fibrinolytic activity in subjects who were over-anxious about taking part in laboratory tests. *Lancet, ii,* 521.

Ratcliffe, H.L. and Cronin, M.T. (1958). Changing frequency of arteriosclerosis in mammals and birds at the Philadelphia Zoological Garden. *Circulation, 18,* 41-52

Ratcliffe, H.L. *et al.* (1960). Changes in the character and location of arterial lesions in mammals and birds in the Philadelphia Zoological Garden. *Circulation, 21*, 730-8

Ratcliffe, H.L. and Snyder, H.L. (1964) Coronary arterial disease with myocardial infarction; a response to social interaction among chickens. *Fed. Prod., 23*, 443

Sikes, S.K. (1969). Habitat and cardiovascular disease: observations made on elephants (*Loxodonta africana*) and other free-living animals in East Africa. *Trans. Zoo. Soc. Lond., 32*, 1, 1-103

BIBLIOGRAPHY

Ashton, E.H., and Zuckerman, S. 'The Effects of Geographic Isolation on the Skull of the Green Monkey *Cercopithecus aethiops sabaeus*', Part I, *Proc. Roy. Soc.*, B, 137 (1950), 212.
——. 'The Effects of Geographic Isolation on the Skull of the Green Monkey *Cercopithecus aethiops sabaeus*', Part II, *Proc. Roy. Soc.*, B, 138 (1951a), 204
——. 'The Effects of Geographic Isolation on the Skull of the Green Monkey *Cercopithecus aethiops sabaeus*', Part III, *Proc. Roy. Soc.*, B, 138 (1951b), 213
——. 'The Effects of Geographic Isolation on the Skull of the Green Monkey *Cercopithecus aethiops sabaeus*', Part IV, *Proc. Roy. Soc.*, B, 138 (1951c), 254
——. 'The Effects of Geographic Isolation on the Skull of the Green Monkey *Cercopithecus aethiops sabaeus*', Part V, *Proc. Roy. Soc.*, B, 151 (1960), 563
Beveridge, W.I.B. *Influenza: The Last Great Plague*. London, Heinemann, 1977.
Bibby, G. *Four Thousand Years Ago: A Panorama of Life in the Second Millennium B.C.* London, Collins, 1962
Bourlière, F. 'Lifespans of Mammalian and Bird Populations in Nature' in Ciba Foundation, *Colloquia on Ageing*. London, J. and A. Churchill, 1959.
Braidwood, R.J. 'The Agricultural Revolution' (1960) in Ehrlich *et al.*, *Man and the Ecosphere*. San Francisco, Freeman, 1971.
Colyer, F. *Variations and Diseases of the Teeth of Animals*. London, Bale and Danielson, 1936
Comfort, A. *Ageing: The Biology of Senescence*. London, Routledge and Kegan Paul, 1956
——. *The Process of Ageing*. London, Weidenfeld and Nicolson, 1965
Deevey, E.S. 'The Human Population' (1960) in Ehrlich *et al.*, *Man and the Ecosphere*. San Francisco Freeman, 1971.
Ehrlich, Paul R. *et al.* (eds.). *Man and the Ecosphere: Readings from Scientific American*. San Francisco, Freeman, 1971
Ernest, M. *The Longer Life*. London, Adam, 1938
Fenner, F. 'Infectious Disease and Social Change', *Med. J. of Australia*, 1, 1043 (15 May 1971), 2, 1099 (22 May 1971)

Hicks, Sir C.S. *Man and Natural Resources.* London, Croom Helm, 1975

Howe, G.M. *Man, Environment and Disease in Britain.* New York, Barnes and Noble; Newton Abbott, David and Charles, 1972

Iverson, J. 'Forest Clearance in the Stone Age' (1956) in Ehrlich *et al., Man and the Ecosphere.* San Francisco, Freeman, 1971.

Manley, G. *Climate and the British Scene.* London, New Naturalist, 1952, 1962 and Fontana, 1970 (new impression)

Montagu, A. *Human Heredity.* New York, Signet Science Library, 1963

Penrose, L.S. *The Biology of Mental Defect.* London, Sidgwick and Jackson, 1963

Roberts, J.C., and Straus, R. (eds.). *Comparative Artherosclerosis.* New York and London, Harper and Row, 1965

Robson, R.K. *Malnutrition: Its Causation and Control.* New York, Gordon and Breach, 2 vols., 1972

INDEX

adenoviruses, 134-5
ageing, processes of, 11-13
agriculture, development of, 23-5
    malpractices, 27-8, 74-5, 77-8
amoebiasis, 40
antigenic drift and shift, 65-6
arterio- and atherosclerosis, 119-28
arthropods in disease transmission,
    31-2, 62-3, 67
asbestosis, 130

baldness, 110-11
battered baby syndrome, 106-7
beri-beri, 56
bilharzia, *vide* schistosomiasis
birds, arterial disease, 123
    cancers of, 133
    influenzas of, 66
breast cancer, 130, 133
Burkitt Lymphoma, 136

cancer, 37-8, 115, 130-40
carbohydrates, 49
carcinogens, 130, 132
cardio-vascular and cerebro-vascular
    diseases, 37, 52, 118-29
carnivores and disease, 40, 134
cataract, 104
cattle and disease, 39
cervical carcinoma (of women), 136
chicken pox, 103
chromosome defects, 112-14
climate and disease, 31-3
coronary thrombosis, *vide* cardio-vas-
    cular and cerebro-vascular disease
cretinism, 102

deserts, encroachment of, 75
diabetes, 100, 102, 109
disease, role in limitation of
    population, 18, 20
diseases, genetic, 100-1
    occupational, 34, 35
    sex-linked, 111-14
dogs and disease, 39-40
Down's Syndrome, *vide* mongolism
drugs in disease control, 31, 34
    effect on foetus, 104-5

ecology of man, cycles in, 72-83
elephants, stress as a cause of cardio-
    vascular disease, 93, 124, 125
energy, uses and development of, 78-
    80
enteric diseases, 34, 40, 68-9, 70-1
environment, man's relations with, 9,
    13, 21-2
environment after birth, effect on new-
    born, 106-8
environment, intra-uterine, effects on
    foetal development, 101-6
erysipelas, 103

fats, saturated and unsaturated, 50-3,
    103
fowl plague, 64
frogs, cancer of, 133-4

gametes, maturation and crossing
    over, 99
genes, 98-100
    dominant and recessive, homozy-
        osity and heterozygosity, 99
    lethal and semi-lethal, 111-12
    genetic defects, 29, 34
    genetic diseases, sex-linked, 110-
        11
    genetic drift, monkeys and man,
        95-7
    genetics and inheritance, 95-117
    genetic unfitness (infertility in
        man), 13, 19, 21
genotype and phenotype, 100-8
German measles, 104
glandular fever, *vide* infectious mono-
    nucleosis
goitre, 36, 102
gout, 111
grains as food, 41-7
Green Revolution, 74

haemophilia, 100
herpesviruses, 38, 40, 132, 136-8
hierarchy, *vide* territory and hierarchy
horses, influenzas of, 65-6
hydatid, 38-9
hydrocephaly, 101